Use LibreOffice Calc

THOMAS ECCLESTONE

ISBN: 1507504225
ISBN-13: 978-1507504222

NONFICTION BOOKS BY AUTHOR

CONTENTS

DEDICATION

This book is dedicated to Kris Rusch for her advice over the years.

1 FIRST STEPS

Why Use LibreOffice Calc?

People often need to work with sheets of figures. For example, where you want to create a basic balance sheet for a business plan, record your expenditures, create time sheets or expense applications.

LibreOffice allows you to quickly create spreadsheets, edit them, and use a powerful array of tools to use them to model the world or run statistical analysis.

And this book will take you from the first stages to a more advanced knowledge of how to use the program.

Step One - Download

1 Go to http://www.LibreOffice.org/download/LibreOffice-fresh/ in your browser

2 Click on the version of LibreOffice that you want to download. The screenshots in this guide are taken from version 4.2.5 for windows.

DOWNLOAD VERSION 4.2.5

3 If using chrome, the following box will appear at the bottom of the screen while the download is taking place. An estimate of how long the download will take is also shown.

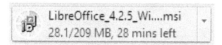

4 Once the download is finished, the following will appear at the bottom of the screen in chrome.

Other web browsers will vary.

Congratulations, you're ready to run the installer!

Step Two - Install

1 Click on the LibreOffice install program. You can either find it at the bottom of your screen in chrome:

Or by opening File Explorer ![file explorer icon] and selecting the download folder:

Use LibreOffice Calc

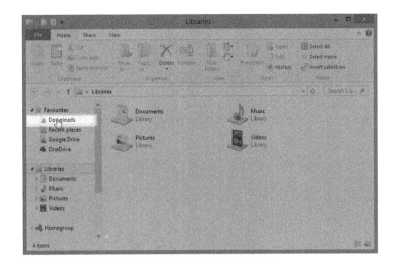

Then double clicking on the installer

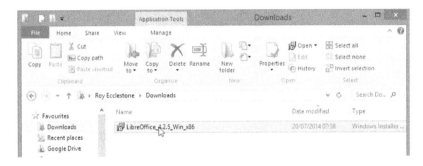

❷ The LibreOffice installation wizard will appear

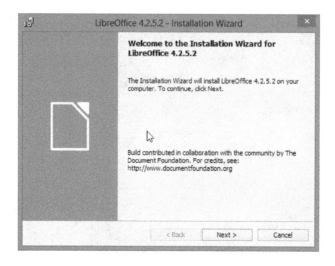

Click on

❸ In the next dialogue you will be given the option of a typical or custom install. I recommend simply using the typical install.

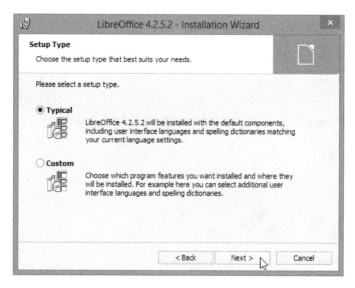

If you are happy with the typical install click

If you want to install a custom installation see "How to run a custom installation" below.

4 The next screen gives you a few more options. I recommend you click on install

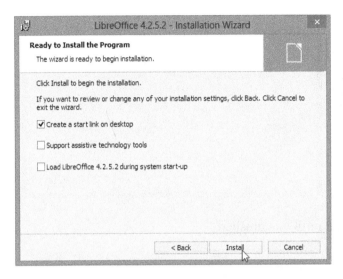

Selecting ☑ Support assistive technology tools will install tools that LibreOffice provides for people with various disabilities.

Selecting ☑ Load LibreOffice 4.2.5.2 during system start-up will mean that LibreOffice will start when the operating system starts. It's useful if you use LibreOffice almost all the time but may slow down loading the operating system.

When you are happy with your options click Install . If you are not happy with any choice you've made you can go back to an earlier choice by clicking < Back .

5 A user account dialogue will appear. Click "Yes", "Allow" or "Ok".

6 A progress dialogue will appear:

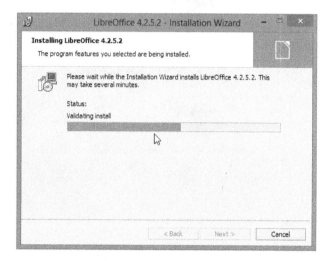

Wait until it is finished

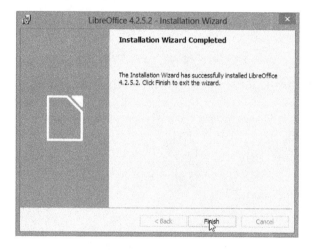

and click on **Finish**.

How to run a custom installation

Run the install procedure above, but in step instead of selecting

Typical

LibreOffice 4.2.5.2 will be installed with the default components, including user interface languages and spelling dictionaries matching your current language settings.

select

Custom

Choose which program features you want installed and where they will be installed. For example here you can select additional user interface languages and spelling dictionaries.

Then click on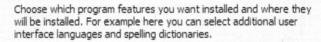

To find out if there is available space for the feature set you've selected click on

The following dialogue will appear:

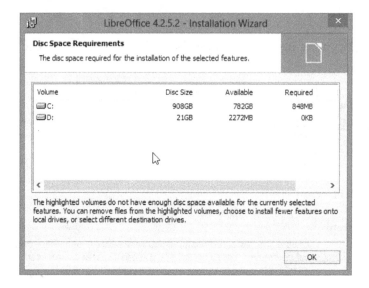

Notice that the column Available shows how much space your disk contains, and Required shows how much disk space your installation has available.

In the above example, we're good to go.

Click [OK] to return to the custom installation dialogue.

❸ To change the location the program will install to select change

A location selection dialogue will appear:

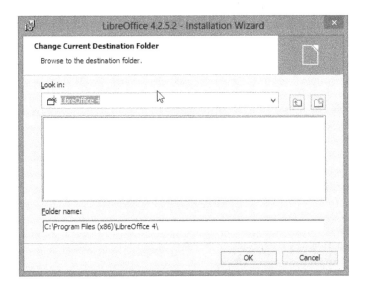

Clicking on the ⌄ next to the look in location will provide you with a list of folders

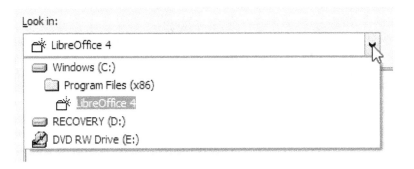

Which you can select from, going up or down as necessary.

You can add a new folder by selecting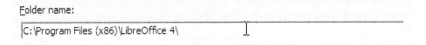

Or you can simply type the file location in the box provided

Folder name:

C:\Program Files (x86)\LibreOffice 4\

I don't recommend changing the file location UNLESS your default drive doesn't have enough room for the installation to work.

❸ To install a new language

Click on the  next to  Additional user interface languages

A list of languages will appear:

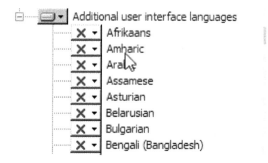

Scroll down to the language you want, and click on the ⟦X ▾⟧

Select ⟦ This feature will be installed on local hard drive. ⟧ if you want it installed on the local hard drive or

⟦ This feature, and all sub-features, will be installed on local hard drive. ⟧ if you want sub features such as spell check and custom fonts to be installed. I recommend this option.

❹ To install non-English language dictionaries:

Click on the ⊞ next to ⊞ ⟦▾⟧ ⟦Optional Components⟧

Click on the ⊞ next to ⊞ ⟦▾⟧ ⟦Dictionaries⟧

Scroll down to the dictionary you want, and click on the ⟦X ▾⟧ by its name, for example:

Select

This feature, and all sub-features, will be installed on local hard drive.

5 Other Optional Components

LibreOffice installs most components by default. The only exception is ActiveX components. If you don't need a particular component and you are low on space you can click the ▭▾ by its name and select **This feature will not be available.** but I do not recommend doing this. It will limit the facilities your LibreOffice installation can provide to you.

Some people may need ActiveX controls, in which case you can select the ✗▾ by **✗▾ ActiveX Control** and **This feature, and all sub-features, will be installed on local hard drive.** . I don't recommend doing this unless you know that you will need ActiveX controls since it can slow down LibreOffice and it's an unusual requirement

6 Once happy with the options you have selected click on **Next >** . A File type dialogue will appear

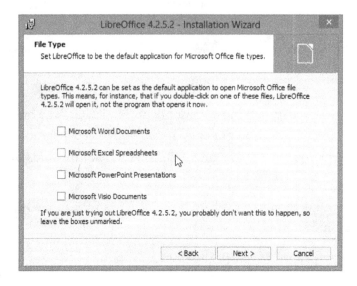

I recommend leaving the defaults on this, but simply check the box next to the file types you want to associate LibreOffice with and click Next > when you are happy.

❼You are now on the installation dialogue that is the last step in "Install LibreOffice" above.

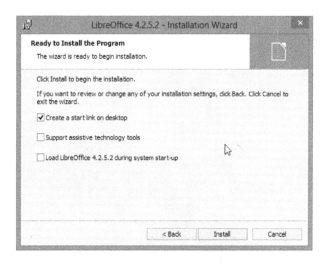

Selecting ☑ Support assistive technology tools will install tools that

LibreOffice provides for people with various disabilities.

Selecting ☑ Load LibreOffice 4.2.5.2 during system start-up will mean that LibreOffice will start when the operating system starts. It's useful if you use LibreOffice almost all the time but may slow down loading the operating system.

When you are happy with your options click Install . If you are not happy with any choice you've made you can go back to an earlier choice by clicking < Back .

❽A user account control dialogue may appear. Click "Ok", "Yes" or "Allow" depending on what version of windows you use.

❾A progress dialogue will appear.

Wait until the installer finishes:

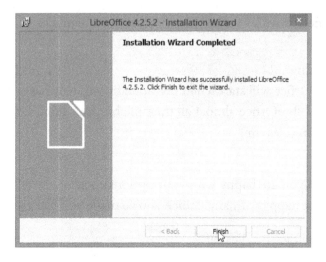

And click on .

To Run

To run LibreOffice Calc double click on its icon on the desktop

 or select its tile in the start screen or search for it.

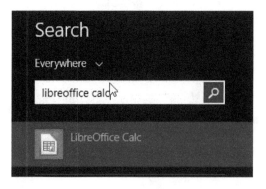

Note that when you open the program via the desktop shortcut you will get the main LibreOffice window whereas if you click on the LibreOffice Calc shortcut you will get the main Calc window.

Create a New Document

If you've started the main LibreOffice program you will see the following window:

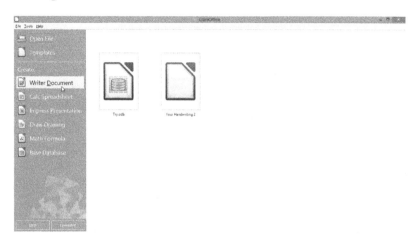

To create a new spreadsheet click on:

To open an existing document

In the main LibreOffice window, click on

Select the file you want to open:

This works the same way that any other open dialogue works. First you select the file directory either using the sidebar or the folder list:

Then you double click on the file that you want to open, or you single click on the file and then click **Open**. Note that often you'll see files of more than one type in the dialogue window. This is inevitable since libreoffice offers such a wide range of suite applications. It can edit word processed documents, databases, and even drawings. In this case we're working on spreadsheet files.

In the above example I'm going to open up a file called Tutorial1 which is an ods file – a LibreOffice Spreadsheet file.

When you double click on the spreadsheet file you'll see the

LibreOffice Calc main window for the first time.

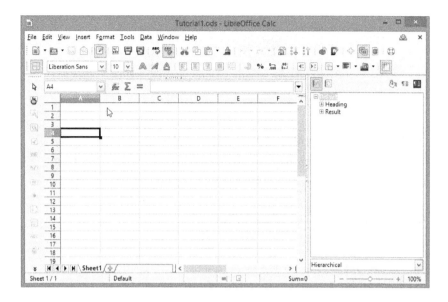

Menu and Toolbars

You can see a fairly complicated looking program. At the top of the screen is a menu bar:

File   Edit   View   Insert   Format   Tools   Data   Window   Help

Under the menu bar is a toolbar which provides a lot of icons that you can use to make LibreOffice Calc do a large range of things very quickly:

Updating the Program

Note also on the right hand corner of the screen is a little icon next to the close button. When LibreOffice has a newer version available this is displayed, and you can update the program.

Note that in the update window you'll see a status indication saying what version is available and what your current installed version is.

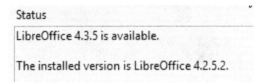

If you want to update LibreOffice click on .
This will take you automatically to a web page where the current
version of the installer is available for download.

Form Controls dockable dialogue

The next thing that you can see varied in terms of placement
depending on your choices. It is a dockable dialogue. In this case for
Form Controls – a form is rather like a specialist program with
buttons, check boxes and so on, which you can use to automatically
update a spreadsheet.

Because it is a dockable dialogue you can move it all over the screen. I like to move it to the left hand side of the screen. You do this by clicking and holding the mouse right at the top edge, then dragging it until you're close up to the edge of the window. In fact your mouse should actually be on the shaded numbers at the left hand of the screen. When you're in the right place you'll see a rectangle around all the numbers:

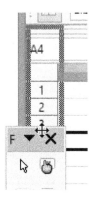

I've suggested moving this dialogue in order to leave the main working area free from distraction. You'll find that since you do the vast majority of your work in this area you will need to leave it free as far as possible.

Formula Bar and location bar

Just above the main working area – which you can also call the spreadsheet – there is a formula bar. LibreOffice calc is a spreadsheet and one of the most powerful features that spreadsheets have is the ability to automatically carry out calculations based on data that you enter into the spreadsheet.

I'll describe these formulas in a lot more detail later on in the book.

Another thing to note is the Name Box which tells you where in the spreadsheet you're currently located.

Spreadsheet View

Below the Formula bar is the spreadsheet itself. At the moment it's empty:

	A	B	C	D	E
1					
2					
3					
4					
5					
6					

The spreadsheet is divided into rows and columns. Notice that the columns start with the letter A, and the rows start with the number 1. Each square is denoted by a combination of letter and number. In the above case we've selected sell A1. There is a rectangle around the square that shows you've selected it.

If you click on cell C3 the highlight will move:

	A	B	C	D
1				
2				
3				
4				
5				
6				

Note also that that in the row and column the appropriate letter for the cell(s) you've highlighted has turned bright blue. And, of course, the Name Box has also changed:

Running a Simple Formula

While it's common to edit data in only one cell at a time it's also not unusual to need to select more than one cell at a time. Here's an example of a very simple spreadsheet:

	A	B
1		Daily Expenses
2		
3		£5.00
4		£2.00
5		£12.00
6		£34.00
7	Total	
8		

If you want to add all the sums together you'd first click on cell B7. Then what? Well, I talked about formulas in the above example. One of these formulas is called SUM. This formula adds up a row of figures.

It's so common in fact that there is a SUM icon on the formula bar. If you click on Σ then LibreOffice will automatically try to determine the range that you want to sum together.

SUM		✓	𝑓x	✗	↵	=SUM(B3:B6)

	A	B
1		Daily Expenses
2		
3		£5.00
4		£2.00
5		£12.00
6		£34.00
7	Total	=SUM(B3:B6)
8		

Note that in cell B7 you see a FORUMLA. In this case it's the SUM formula, and you are adding together cells B3 to B6 inclusive. The cells in the range are highlighted with a blue border.

Note that =SUM( ) is a formula, and the thing within the brackets is a parameter. In this case the parameter is a RANGE.

When you're happy with a formula press ENTER. You'll see the result of the formula in the cell:

B8	☑	*fx* Σ =	
	A	B	C
1		Daily Expenses	
2			
3		£5.00	
4		£2.00	
5		£12.00	
6		£34.00	
7	Total	£53.00	
8			
9			

But clicking back onto the cell will display the formula again, allowing you to edit it if you want.

Note also that when you change one of the cells that the formula depends on the formula will be recalculated automatically and the result in the cell will change automatically too:

	A	B
1		Daily Expenses
2		
3		£105.00
4		£2.00
5		£12.00
6		£34.00
7	Total	£153.00
8		

Which is one of the main strengths of a spreadsheet application. The ability to see what happens if you change a few details in a spreadsheet actually provides a huge amount of power when you want to run simulations of crunch figures.

Wow, just in this small section we've covered a lot of ground so don't be surprised if it's a little confusing at the moment.

Cell and Page Styles

On the right hand side of the screen you'll see the Styles dockable window. You can use this to update the look of a cell or a page in order to make the chart look consistent.

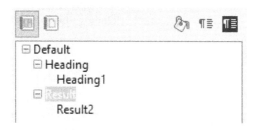

Click onto the cell whose style you want to change. For example, B7 earlier:

| B7 | | ✔ | f_x Σ = | = SUM(B3:B6) |

	A	B	C
1		Daily Expenses	
2			
3		£105.00	
4		£2.00	
5		£12.00	
6		£34.00	
7	Total	£153.00	
8			
9			

Note that the cell becomes highlighted, and you can see the formula that you entered in the formula bar.

In the Style Properties dialogue double click on the style that you want to use. In this case, Result. You'll see that the style that you choose becomes highlighted

And that the appearance of the cell itself changes:

	A	B
1		Daily Expenses
2		
3		£105.00
4		£2.00
5		£12.00
6		£34.00
7	Total	*£153.00*
8		

Sheets tab

You've worked with a simple spreadsheet above, but LibreOffice can handle a number of spreadsheets in each file. For example, dealing with different projects or employees or even weeks in each spreadsheet.

Clicking on a sheet in the spreadsheet tab opens up the sheet for editing.

Clicking on ⊕ adds a new spread sheet.

Saving a File

To save a file click on 🖫 in the toolbar. If you haven't named the file yet, you'll need to save as. You can do this by clicking on

Save As...   Ctrl+Shift+S

in the file menu. This will open a save as dialogue which will be very familiar to you. You can choose the directory in the normal way:

« Google Drive ▸ Tom ▸ NEA

And you can also change the file name:

File name: Tutorial1

This works the same way as any other save as dialogue.

Closing down the Program

Once you're happy that you've saved everything you want to keep, click on Exit LibreOffice   Ctrl+Q in the File Menu to exit LibreOffice.

Next Chapter

In this chapter I've covered the basic information needed to install LibreOffice Calc, and I've also shown you a first spread sheet and a very commonly used function.

The next chapter will be a beginner's tutorial which will show you a lot of the information you need to get early results out of the program.

2 A BASIC TUTORIAL

In this chapter I'm going to produce a couple of basic spreadsheets. The first one of these spreadsheets will be a basic accounting spreadsheet called a profit and loss spreadsheet. I hope that this tutorial will teach you a lot about how to create your own customised spreadsheets.

While the profit and loss statement is a useful financial tool, I'm not a chartered accountant so you'd probably be better off hiring one if you want to do a serious profit and loss sheet. The purpose of this tutorial is just to teach you the rudiments of LibreOffice Calc.

Creating a new Spreadsheet

To create a new spreadsheet click on don't forget to save the spreadsheet first by clicking on Save As... Ctrl+Shift+S in the file menu and saving it.

Renaming the worksheet

Right click on the worksheet name that you're editing in the worksheet tab at the bottom of the screen you'll see a context sensitive menu. Click on Rename Sheet... to give the worksheet a sensible name. This will bring up the Rename Sheet dialogue. Chose an appropriate name for your worksheet.

Name

Profit and Loss

OK

Click when you're happy with the worksheet name. You'll see that the sheet changes name in the worksheet tab:  .

Creating a heading

A heading is effectively just text. You can enter text by clicking into a cell with the mouse.

	A	B	C
1			
2		Tutorial on Profit and Loss	

Note that as you type the text it appears on the screen. When you're editing text you can choose whether to commit the changes or not. Note that the text that you're entering also appears in the

function bar with a big red cross. ✕ ↵ Tutorial   If you click on the ✕ you'll see that the changes you make are rolled back. You can also roll the changes back by pressing the escape key (esc) which is often found on the top left hand of the keyboard.

To commit a change (or in other words, to decide that you want to make a change) you can press ENTER to move down to the next cell.

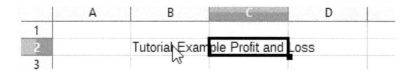

	A	B	C	D
1				
2		Tutorial Example Profit and Loss		
3				
4				

Alternatively, if you click the tab (often found above the caps lock key on the keyboard) you'll commit the change and move to the next cell in the row.

	A	B	C	D
1				
2		Tutorial Example Profit and Loss		
3				

Here's an interesting thing. If you start to type something into the next cell what happens?

	A	B	C	D
1				
2		Tutorial Exam	1.2Loss	
3				

At first, what you're adding appears in the new cell, but the rest of the text is still visible. Once you commit the change by pressing enter you'll see that the text in the new cell hides all of the overflow from the text in the old cell.

	A	B	C	D
1				
2		Tutorial Exam	1.2	
3				
4				

You can resize cells, but it's often a good idea to make sure that if you're going to have a cell with a lot of text in it you keep adjacent cells clear of important text.

Adding a Header Style to the Cell

It's important to style text like headers so that it stands out. Click onto the cell that contains the header. Then, in the style properties on the right hand side double click on Heading

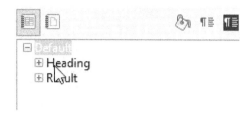

When you do that something odd happens. You see the text that you've entered change to a different alignment, centred, which means that you half the text spills over into the cells before the one that you've just entered:

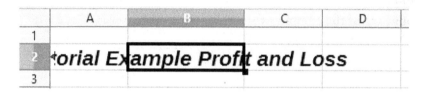

In the toolbar there are a range of Alignment Options that you can choose from ⊞ ⊞ ⊞ ⊞ . If you click on ⊞ it will align the text to the left.

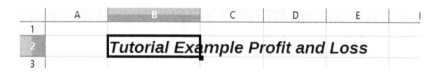

It might help to mention at this point that you're just changing the individual instance in this case rather than the style. I'll show you how to modify styles later on.

You can continue to add text by clicking on a square and typing into it:

	Tutorial Example F
	Total Revenue
Less	Costs of Goods Sold
	Gross Profit

So far we've just entered text. In cell B5 (Costs of Goods Sold) we've hit a problem. The text is a little too large for the sheet. So when we enter text into the next cell it'll obscure the heading.

Resizing a column or row isn't difficult. Move the mouse up to the letter or across to the number which you want to resize. The mouse will change. Click and hold on the mouse, then drag the boundary of the column of the row to the correct place.

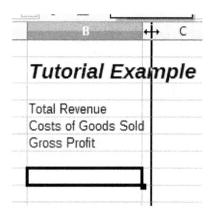

The line will show you where you've resized the column or row _to_. You can use the same process to increase or decrease the width of a cell too.

Entering Numbers

So far we've entered a lot of text data. But the fundamental purpose of most spreadsheets is to crunch numbers. So it's not a surprise that it's easy to enter numerical data too.

Click onto the cell that you want to enter the data into.

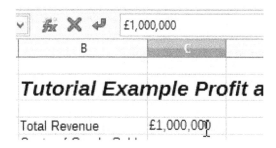

Type in the number. In this example I've used a format – commas to denote millions and thousands. LibreOffice Calc gives you a lot of control over the way that you enter and display numbers. When I press enter to commit the change something odd happens:

Help! Well, not, it's nothing to worry about. When you're entering a number and it's too large to see in the cell you get symbols that show there is a number in the cell – three hash signs.

If you resize the cell you see that the numbers are still there!

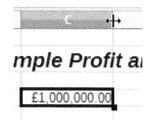

Formatting a Number

In the above example we can see the number is almost written the way we wanted it. But LibreOffice Calc is insisting on showing the decimal points. It's pretty easy to make LibreOffice format a cell the way you want it.

Right click on the cell and select Format Cells... .

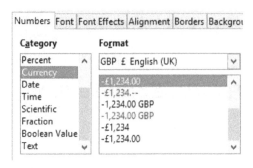

In this case you see that there are a lot of format options including Percent, Currency, Date, Time and so on. But LibreOffice has detected that this cell is probably a currency cell, and that it is probably British Pounds. You can click on another option to override this default. But in this case LibreOffice has detected the right basic format (it's a number in GBP) but we want to select one of the other options. Note also that there are black options and red ones. Sometimes people like to denote a negative number in red. If you choose one of the red options and there is a loss it will show up in red.

In this case I select -£1,234 which produces a format the way that I want it.

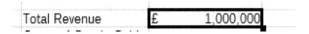

Selecting a range of cells

Sometimes you may want to format more than one sell at a time. To do this, click on the first cell of the range and then hold the mouse button. Move the mouse to the last cell of the range. You'll see all the cells you've chosen highlighted.

Tutorial Example Profit and I

Total Revenue	£1,000,000
Costs of Goods Sold	
Gross Profit	

Let go of the mouse. Now, right click on any of the highlighted cells and select Format Cells... to change the formatting.

When you're doing a lot of cells at once you'll often find that it's necessary to select the category in the Format Cells dialogue manually. Just click on the category for the formatting that you want.

Category

Number
Percent
Currency
Date
Time

We continue entering the data.

	Total Revenue	£1,000,000
Less	Costs of Goods Sold	£400,000
	Gross Profit	

A basic Calculation

Obviously, now we've got to Gross Profit. Which is Total Revenue minus Cost of Goods Sold in this case. *I could just type in a number after doing the calculation.* That might even be a 'sensible' approach. But it's much easier to get LibreOffice to do the work of calculating the answer for me.

Calculations start with the symbol =. So type in =

Gross Profit	=

Then move the mouse to C4 (total revenue) and click on it once.

Total Revenue	£1,000,000
Costs of Goods Sold	£400,000
Gross Profit	=C4

Note that the cell number appears in the formula, and you see a purple rectangle around the cell.

We're taking away (subtracting). So we type in - . Then Click on the cell we're taking away C5 (Cost of Goods Sold).

Total Revenue	£1,000,000
Costs of Goods Sold	£400,000
Gross Profit	=C4-C5

And press enter. LibreOffice Calc does the calculation for you automatically.

Total Revenue	£1,000,000
Costs of Goods Sold	£400,000
Gross Profit	£600,000

That may seem a little bit of a palaver. But because we're using a formula if we change either the Total Revenue or Costs of Goods Sold the calculation is updated automatically for us.

Making a cell Bold

The Gross Profit cell is an important cell. One way that you can make an important cell stand out is to bold it. Click onto cell C6 and then click bold A to emphasise the cell.

Tutorial Example Profit and Loss

	Total Revenue	£1,000,000
Less	Costs of Goods Sold	£400,000
	Gross Profit	£600,000

A Percentage Calculation

In the above example we've already used a simple formula – a subtraction. You can also produce a percentage to find out what percentage of total revenue the costs of goods sold are.

Click onto cell D5. You can repeat the same process with the mouse button to get the following formula:

> =C5/C4*100

Note that there are two mathematical symbols here. / which means division, and * which means multiplication.

In this case it means Costs of Goods Sold divided by Total Revenue then multiplied by a 100. The order of operational precedence is similar to the mathematics that you learned at school. One thing to note is that you can use brackets ( ) to change the order of precedence:

> =C5/(C4*100)

Is a very different calculation than the one above. In the first example you calculate c5 divided by c4 first, then multiply by 100. In the second example you calculate C4*100 first, then divide c5 by the answer.

Another thing… when we finish our calculation we see:

	Total Revenue	£1,000,000	
Less	Costs of Goods Sold	£400,000	£40
	Gross Profit	£600,000	

LibreOffice has decided that since the calculation is all based on Currency, the result is probably a currency. Format the cell by right clicking on it, and then choosing Format Cells... .

In the categories click on Percent and then choose the type of format for percent that you want. In this case I've decided to go for two decimal places. -13% / -12.95% Then Click OK . When you check out the spreadsheet you quickly see the marvelous result of your calculation... an error:

Costs of Goods Sold	£400,000	4000.00%

Why? Well, when LibreOffice sees a cell that is a percentage it automatically multiplies it by a hundred. So the formula you want for this cell is actually slightly more simple than the one we included above. The correct calculation is =C5/C4 .

We can repeat the process to calculate the Gross Profit Percentage. =C6/C4 .

D6			fx Σ =	=C6/C4		
	A	B		C	D	E
1						
2		**Tutorial Example Profit and Loss**				
3						
4		Total Revenue		£1,000,000		
5	Less	Costs of Goods Sold		£400,000	40.00%	
6		Gross Profit		£600,000	60.00%	

A simple Pie Chart

While not *strictly speaking* something that often appears on a profit and loss statement, sometimes it can help people visualise data if they have a chart. So, highlight the items that you want to include in the chart:

Total Revenue	£1,000,000	
Costs of Goods Sold	£400,000	40.00%
Gross Profit	£600,000	60.00%

Then click on the Chart icon in the toolbar. You'll see the Chart Wizard. I'll describe it in more detail later on in the book, but for the moment we're going to create a pie chart. Click on Pie in the categories list.

Choose the style of pie chart that you want to use (in this case I'm going with the default)

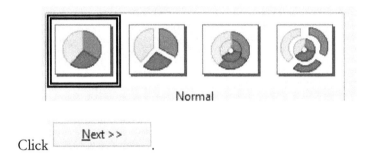

Normal

Click Next >> .

You'll see a data range:

Data range

S'Profit and Loss'.$B$5:$C$6

This looks a little complicated. The first section is the worksheet, the second section after the '.' is a cell range.

But you can usually just use one of the options

○ Data series in rows or ● Data series in columns

Click [Next >>] to open the Data Series task in the Chart

Wizard. I'll explain that later. Just click on [Next >>] for now.

Type in the Title for the chart

Title | Gross Profit and Cost of Goods

Click on the rectangle ☑ Display legend if you don't want to display the legend. You can also change the position of the legend my selecting one of the other options.

○ Left

● Right

○ Top

○ Bottom

Once you're happy with your selections click

on [Finish] .

You'll see a chart appear. You can move the chart by moving the mouse to the border of the chart (the mouse will change to a little

cross ✛) then clicking and holding the mouse button and then dragging it to wherever you want it on the worksheet.

Around the chart are a number of small rectangles. When you move your mouse over the rectangles on the corner of the chart it

changes to arrows. ⬉ Click and hold the mouse, then drag it in the direction of the arrows (i.e. towards the centre of the object to make it smaller, or away to make it larger).

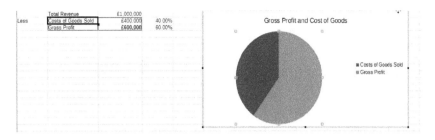

Completing the expense section.

So far we've filled out part of the spreadsheet. We've edited cells to include text, formatted cells to include numbers, and we've also created a simple chart. We've learned most of the functions you need to create simple spreadsheets.

For example, we know how to add the following to the spreadsheet:

8	Less	Expenses		
9		Accounting and Legal	£	50,000
10		Advertising	£	150,000
11		Depreciation	£	89,000
12		Training	£	45,000
13	Less	Total Expenses		
14	Equals	Net Profit		
15				

Remember, you click into a cell to edit the content. If you type text you can format it using the bold icon on the task bar . You can enter a number with a currency symbol. If you want you can format the number by right clicking on a cell, or selecting a range of cells and then right clicking on it to format multiple cells.

Doing the calculations: Total Expenses

The first calculation is to work out Total Expenses. Click on the cell and then the SUM function icon Σ to select the range of cells.

8	Less	Expenses		
9		Accounting and Legal	£	50,000
10		Advertising	£	150,000
11		Depreciation	£	89,000
12		Training	£	45,000
13	Less	Total Expenses	=SUM(C9:C12)	

You can press enter.

Doing the Calculations: Net profit

Remember from earlier that to create a calculation you need to enter the cell where you want to display the calculation, type in = and then enter the formula that you want the spread sheet to calculate.

For Net Profit the formula is Gross Profit – Total Expenses.

First click into the cell, then type =. Use the mouse to select the cell that has gross profit (C6).

		Total Revenue		£1,000,000	
	Less	Costs of Goods Sold		£400,000	40.00%
		Gross Profit		£600,000	60.00%
	Less	Expenses			
		Accounting and Legal	£	50,000	
		Advertising	£	150,000	
		Depreciation	£	89,000	
		Training	£	45,000	
	Less	Total Expenses	£	334,000	
	Equals	Net Profit	=C6		

Then use the operator – and click on the Cell that contains Total expenses

13	Less	Total Expenses	£	334,000
14	Equals	Net Profit	=C6-C13	
15				

When you press enter the calculation will be performed. Here's something that I always advise: when you're doing a calculation like this for the first time just check the sums mentally to see if it makes sense.

Less	Total Expenses	£	334,000
Equals	Net Profit		£266,000

In this case our mental calculation looks about right.

We can do percentages like we did before. For example Total Expenses as a percentage of Total revenue:

Less	Total Expenses	£	334,000 =C13/C4

Remembering to format the cell as a percentage using the right mouse button.

Editing a Cell with a Formula

To edit a cell with a formula double click on it. Note that when you do this LibreOffice gives you a hint about what cells belong to what item in the formula – the colour of a cell reference in the formula is the same as the highlight colour around the cell.

Equals	Net Profit	£	£266,000 =C14/C4

Inserting Rows or Columns into a Spreadsheet

Life would be simpler if we could just enter data into a spreadsheet once and it always remained the same. But you'll find that in reality you're always adding new information to a spreadsheet. For example, in this tutorial we've got a number of expenses listed. But maybe the management decides to pay itself a salary. You're going to have to include the figure in your profit and loss account.

To insert a row into a spreadsheet the first step is to right click on the cell below where you want to insert the row.

For example if you want to insert a row between 8 and 9, right click on 9:

8	Less	Expenses		
9		Accounting and Legal	£	50,000
10		Advertising	£	150,000
11		Depreciation	£	89,000

Then click on ⊞ Insert Rows Above . You'll immediately see a new row above the row you selected. The row is empty.

8	Less	Expenses		
9				
10		Accounting and Legal	£	50,000
11		Advertising	£	150,000

Type in the new Director Salary information.

Less	Expenses	
	Director Salary	

Note that the row takes on the formatting of the row that is directly above it. So you'll have to change any formatting that you might want. In this case you'll also see that the new line isn't included in your calculation:

8	Less	Expenses		
9		Director Salary	£	24,000
10		Accounting and Legal	£	50,000
11		Advertising	£	150,000
12		Depreciation	£	89,000
13		Training	£	45,000
14	Less	Total Expenses	=SUM(C10:C13)	

Change it manually in this case.

Total Expenses =SUM(C9:C13)

Inserting a row in the middle of a range

In the above example we inserted a row above the range. If, however, we were to insert a row in the middle of the range (say, above row 12) we get a slightly different result:

8	Less	Expenses		
9		Director Salary	£	24,000
10		Accounting and Legal	£	50,000
11				
12		Advertising	£	150,000
13		Depreciation	£	89,000
14		Training	£	45,000
15	Less	Total Expenses	=SUM(C9:C14)	

The new row is automatically included in the Total Expenses formula. You don't have to manually change the formula to include the fact that you've added a new row. Say you then add a Postal bill, the calculation automatically adjusts to the figure you've added.

Less	Expenses			
	Director Salary	£	24,000	
	Accounting and Legal	£	50,000	
	Postal	£	14,000	
	Advertising	£	150,000	
	Depreciation	£	89,000	
	Training	£	45,000	
Less	Total Expenses	£	372,000	37.20%

If you insert a row ABOVE the rows effected by a formula the formula will automatically update so that it still refers to the same cells. Say, for example, you add another row above row 7:

7				
8				
9	Less	Expenses		
10		Director Salary	£	24,000
11		Accounting and Legal	£	50,000
12		Postal	£	14,000
13		Advertising	£	150,000
14		Depreciation	£	89,000
15		Training	£	45,000
16	Less	Total Expenses	=SUM(C10:C15)	37.20%
17	Equals	Net Profit	£228,000	22.80%

The range in cell C16 is automatically updated. But also the percentage in D16 is automatically updated to reflect the changes you've made to the work sheet.

While these automatic function reference updates generally behave intuitively, when you're inserting a row or a column it's generally worth making sure that you check that any functions that you've made are still 'sensible.'

Seeing which cells are based on calculations

If you click on ⎸ Value **H**ighlighting Ctrl+F8 ⎸ in the View Menu all cells that are based on calculations will appear in green. All other cells will be blue. Click on it again to return to the normal view.

Inserting a column

It's basically the same procedure to insert a column as to insert a row. You right click on the column header to the right of where you want to insert the column, and then click ⎸ **I**nsert Columns Left ⎸ .

	B	C	D
	Tutorial Example Profit and Loss		
	Total Revenue		£1,000,000
	Costs of Goods Sold		£400,000
	Gross Profit		£600,000

Note that the calculations that you've made are automatically adjusted to cope with the fact you've created a new column in the same way they would if you inserted a row.

Deleting a Column or Row

Right click on the column or row header for the row that you want to delete. Then, in the case of columns click

on 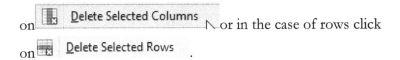 or in the case of rows click

on ![Delete Selected Rows icon] Delete Selected Rows .

Note that you can delete more than one row or column at a time by left clicking the first row or column you want to select, holding the mouse button down, and moving to the final column or row you want to select.

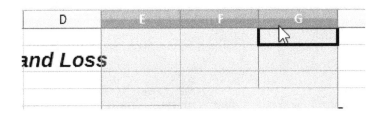

Then right click within the highlighted area in the row or column header as above.

Cut, Copy and Paste

It's pretty easy to cut, copy or paste a row, column or range of cells. First you have to select the items you want to cut or copy. If it's a row or column select them using the header – i.e. click with the left mouse button and hold then move to the end of the selection.

If it's a cell you move to the first cell in the range you want to select, click and hold, then move the mouse to the opposite corner of the range you want to select.

After that it's easy. Right click on your selection and then choose ![Cut icon] Cut if you want to remove the cells after copying them to the clipboard:

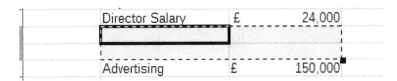

Or 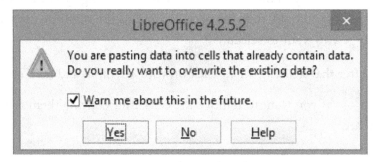 **Copy**   if you just want to copy the cells to the clipboard:

9		Director Salary	£	24,000
10		Accounting and Legal	£	50,000
11		Postal	£	14,000
12		Advertising	£	150,000

Note that if you cut you may want to remove the cells altogether, in which case you may want to right click on the area and choose Delete... then select which direction you want to shift the cells.

Paste

Ordinarily pasting is a simple matter of right clicking where you want to insert the data you've copied and then selecting **Paste** . For example, if you're pasting a column right click on the column where you want the content pasted and then click **Paste** . The content of the clipboard will be pasted to the column which you've selected.

And this will work. However, it will replace everything in the location where you're copying the data and you'll get the following warning:

LibreOffice 4.2.5.2 ✕

⚠ You are pasting data into cells that already contain data.
Do you really want to overwrite the existing data?

☑ Warn me about this in the future.

    Yes   No   Help

If you want to paste cells, rows or columns without losing the existing data you've got to be a bit more sneaky about matters. Select the cells, rows or column where you want to insert the data and then

48

click on Paste Special...   .

There are a lot of options here that I'll describe in more detail, but the one that you want is Shift Cells. If you select Don't Shift (the default) you'll overwrite the cells that you've chosen. If you select Right or Down you'll insert new cells to the right or above the cell(s) you've selected.

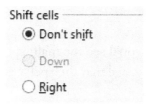

You'll see a number of other options in this Paste Special link. In the main they work as you'd expect, but I'll get back to them later on.

Running a Spell Check

When you're working on a spreadsheet it's easy to make a spelling mistake. LibreOffice Calc runs an automated spell check all the time, highlighting errors in spelling using an underline:

Costs of Goodss Sold

It can be easy to miss a spelling mistake even though it's highlighted. So before printing out a document run a spell check by clicking on ᴬᴮᶜ .

Sometimes when you click on the spell check button LibreOffice won't find any errors after the point you've currently selected on the sheet:

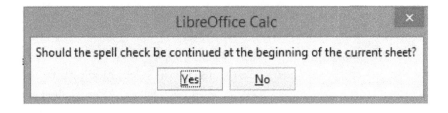

In which case click **Yes** to check the rest of the document.

If there is an error you'll see the main spell checking dialogue. You can choose the language that the spell checker is checking **English (UK)** and see the text immediately around the error:

As well as a list of suggestions:

Suggestions
Goods
Goods s
Godhoods
Gooders
Goodich

Double click on the correct suggestion from the list to choose it, you can also choose to ignore the error once or every time you see it. If the "error" is actually correct you can add it to your own custom dictionary. LibreOffice treats words that you add to the Dictionary as if they are correct – so be careful!

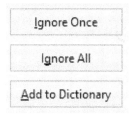

Once you've gone through the entire document deciding whether to correct or ignore errors you'll see LibreOffice tell you that the spell check is complete:

Don't forget to save the document once you're happy with it by clicking on the 🖫 icon in the toolbar.

Page Preview

Before you print out a workbook it's often advised to make sure that you carry out a print preview. While you can print out the workbook simply by pressing 🖶 in the toolbar this carries the risk that you can end up printing a lot of information that you don't want to print.

Instead press Page Preview in the toolbar 🔍.

This will open up the page preview. The main window will display a picture of the page that you're going to print. One thing that it's particularly important to check is at the bottom left hand side of the screen. This shows the current page and the total number of pages that you're going to print

You can sometimes end up printing a lot more pages than you expected if, for example, your worksheet covers several pages.

Once you've checked that you aren't printing huge numbers of pages take a look at the preview window:

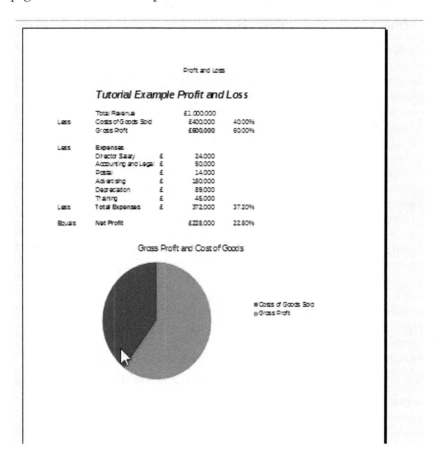

You can scroll through the pages of the worksheet that you are printing using the toolbar. Click on to go to the next page, and to go to the previous page.

If you're happy with the worksheet you're going to print, click

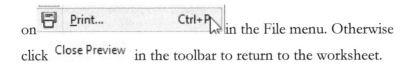 on in the File menu. Otherwise click Close Preview in the toolbar to return to the worksheet.

Printing

The Printing Dialogue is pretty sensible and obvious. Firstly, make sure that you select the right printer from the list of printers that it gives you:

You can alter printer properties using 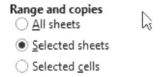 .

You can choose what area to print out using the range and copies. If you've selected an area of cells, choose Selected Cells. Otherwise, to print out the sheet you're currently working on use Selected Sheets.

Range and copies
○ All sheets
◉ Selected sheets
○ Selected cells

I really don't suggest using All Sheets since this can result in printing out a lot of pages that you won't want to print.

Once you've chosen the Range of items to print, you can restrict it further to specific pages. For example in our work sheet we might just want to print out the first page:

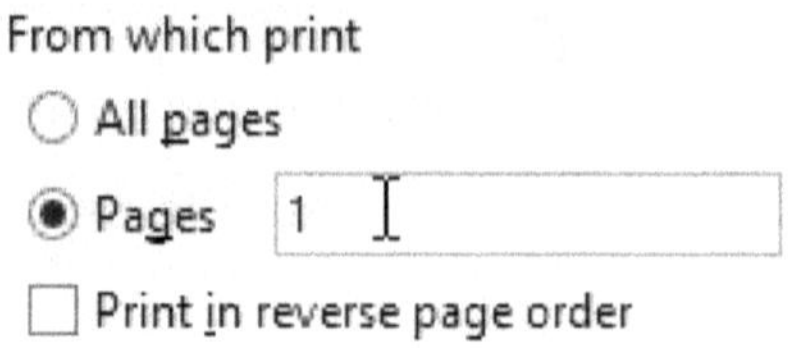
From which print
All pages
Pages 1
Print in reverse page order

You can include ranges in the Pages section by using the dash (i.e. 1-2 is pages 1 and 2 inclusive), and separate selections using the comma (i.e. 1,3-4 prints out pages 1,3,4) noting that if the same page is included more than once it'll be printed out more than once (i.e. 1,1-2 would print out pages 1,1,2)

Finally set the number of copies to print 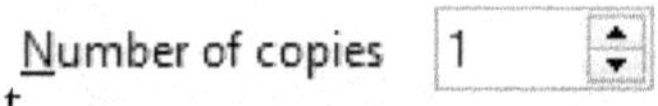
Number of copies 1
and whether you want to collate the pages, then check the preview on the left hand side of the dialogue and click 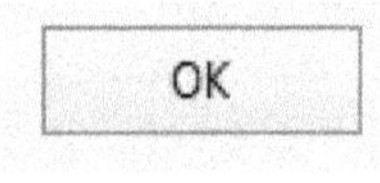
OK
when you're happy.

Finding items in the Spreadsheet

Sometimes when you have a very large spreadsheet you may want to find a specific item in it. Click on 
Find... Ctrl+F
in the edit menu. You'll see the Find Taskbar at the bottom of the screen:

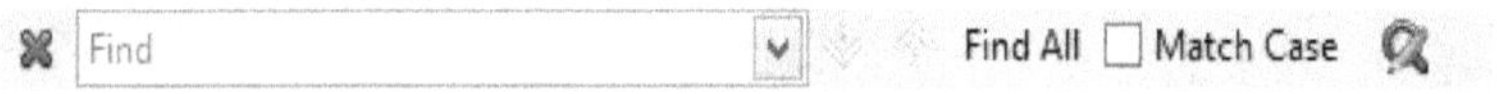
Find
Find All
Match Case

You can press  to close the taskbar. Type the text that you want to find in the Find Box. LibreOffice will search through the file, and if it doesn't find anything it'll ask you if you want to continue from the beginning.

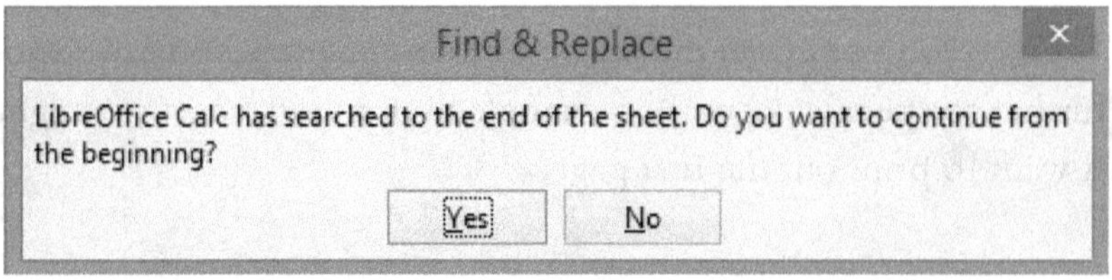
Find & Replace
LibreOffice Calc has searched to the end of the sheet. Do you want to continue from the beginning?
Yes
No

Click on  . The cell that it finds will be highlighted:

Total Revenue	£1,000,000
Costs of Goods Sold	£400,000
Gross Profit	£600,000
Expenses	

You can navigate through the document to the next and previous found items using the buttons provided ⌄ ⌃ or click Find All to display a dialogue showing all the instances. (For example searching for the word Profit)

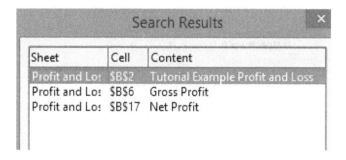

Search Results

Sheet	Cell	Content
Profit and Los	$B$2	Tutorial Example Profit and Loss
Profit and Los	$B$6	Gross Profit
Profit and Los	$B$17	Net Profit

Double click on one of the instances to go to it.

Use Close if you want to leave the Search Results dialogue.

You can match only items of a specific case by clicking on the rectangle next to ☐Match Case .

If you want to replace items click on 🔍 . This brings up the Find and Replace dialogue. One thing to note about this dialogue is that there are two sections. The first section is the find section:

Search for

Enter the text to find. If you click on ⎡Find⎤ you'll go to the next cell with the text that you're searching for. Using

⎡Find All⎤ will select all instances of the searched text. The instance that you've selected is visible on the workbook because it has a bold rectangle around it.

| Equals | Net Profit | £228 |

Once you've got to the first item that you want to replace, type in the replacement text into the appropriate box:

Replace with

If you hit ⎡Replace⎤ it will replace only the item that you've currently selected. ⎡Replace All⎤ Will replace all the selected items.

There are some options that you can use to control if you want to only match items of exactly the same case (i.e. the word "This" and "this" wouldn't match) ☐Match case or match only cells with the exact content ☐Entire cells .

There are also some more advanced options that you can use by clicking on ⊞ Other Options . I'll describe these in detail later on.

Note that using a combination of Find to choose each item, and replace when you want to change a specific item you can have a reasonable amount of control over the items you want to replace. If you don't want to replace an item just click find to go to the next item.

Next Chapter

This chapter has included a basic tutorial that shows you how to add data, create simple formulas, save, print, select, insert and delete cells, and a lot more.

In the next chapter I'm going to go into more detail about functions and calculations.

3 FUNCTIONS AND CALCULATIONS

So far we've already seen some basic calculations in use. When you start editing a cell with the symbol = you're telling LibreOffice Calc to run a calculation. For example the calculation:

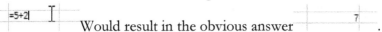

Would result in the obvious answer .

We've also see that we can use sums from other cells as part of the calculation:

We can build on these principals. For example, it's possible to reference a cell in another worksheet:

For example, consider that we've got a spreadsheet where the worksheets include one that we've called Profit and Loss

If we click on Sheet2 and want to refer to a cell that is in the worksheet Profit and Loss we can do so by including the name of the worksheet as a reference:

The name of the worksheet is in single quotes. Then there is a full stop, and the name of the cell within the worksheet. You can do calculations with the result in exactly the same way as a normal cell. For example to find out the average monthly gross profit:

f_x ✗ ↵ ┃ ='Profit and Loss'.C6/12

Preventing LibreOffice Calc treating mathematical text as a calculation

Sometimes you may not want LibreOffice to treat something that looks like a calculation as if it were actually a calculation. For example if you enter:

f_x Σ = ┃ =2+2

It will produce the result `4` when you want to display `=2+2`. You can prevent this from happening by formatting the cell to a text cell BEFORE you enter anything into the cell.

Right click into the cell and select Format Cells... then scroll down in the Category window until you see Text. Double click on it.

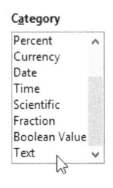

Category

| Percent |
| Currency |
| Date |
| Time |
| Scientific |
| Fraction |
| Boolean Value |
| Text |

And then click on OK . You can then enter the text as

normal.

Basic Functions

While I'm going to go into some detail about functions in general later on in the book there are some functions that are used so often that LibreOffice makes them directly available from the Name Box. When you click into a cell and either press $\equiv$ in the function bar or type = on the keyboard you'll see the following option appear in the Name Box:

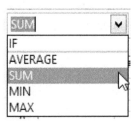

We've already seen the Sum function before – which is a function that finds the total of a range of cells by adding them together.

Finding the (Median) Average Value of a range of Cells

To find the average value of a range of cells type the = symbol then click on AVERAGE in the Name Box:

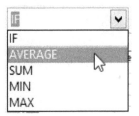

You'll see the AVERAGE function appear in the cell =AVERAGE() select the range of cells you want. This is done by clicking and holding the mouse button in the first cell of the range then dragging the mouse down to the end of the range.

Note you can type the range in the format FIRST CELL: LAST CELL too.

Then press enter.

Finding the Minimum Value or a range of Cells

Finding the minimum value (i.e. lowest value) from a range of cells can be done with the MIN function. Type = as normal, then in the Name Box select MIN ▼ . You'll see the MIN function appear in the cell:

=MIN()

Select the range in the normal way:

When you press ENTER, LibreOffice will select the minimum number from the range of cells.

Finding the Maximum Value of a range of Cells

This is done with the MAX function. Type = and then select MAX ▼ in the Name Box. You can then select the range of cells:

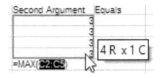

One thing that I may not have made clear so far is that a range of cells can include more than one column:

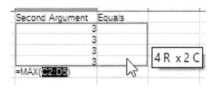

To be honest I don't normally use this functionality but it is there.

Combining functions

Say you want to find the proportion of the contribution of the LOWEST value in a list to the TOTAL VALUE (not something that you'll probably need to do often, but it might come in useful in some forms of statistical analysis).

You can combine functions together using mathematical operators in an intuitive way:

=MIN(C2:C5)/SUM(C2:C5)

IF function – A basic Conditional Function

As we'll see later in the book, LibreOffice Calc offers lots of basic logical functions that allow you a fine control over how the program runs. But one of the most common functions that you'll use is the IF function.

So… let's go back a bit. What's a logical function?

Well, Computing is generally largely based statements like:

IF something is true AND something else is true THEN do

something.

So, IF you're hungry AND there is cake THEN you should eat cake.

OR IF you're hungry OR you're thirsty THEN you should go to the kitchen.

Obviously, that's a real world example of an IF statement. In LibreOffice Calc there are a whole lot of these logical functions – or functions that work on BOOLEAN values. A BOOLEAN value is a value that's either TRUE or FALSE.

The most commonly used Logical Function is probably the IF function. And you can access it from the Name Box in the same way as SUM, AVERAGE, MIN and MAX by typing = and then selecting

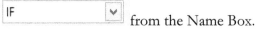 from the Name Box.

The structure of the IF formula is

IF (CONDITION, THEN_VALUE, OTHERWISE_VALUE)

CONDITION is the test that is going to be performed. LibreOffice Calc will do a logical calculation that will produced a true or false value. If the CONDITION is true then the result of the IF statement will be THEN_VALUE, otherwise it will be OTHERWISE_VALUE.

Here is an example of the structure in action. IF cell A2 is equal to 2 then the output for the formula is 1, otherwise it is 3.

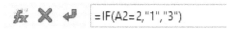

Would produce the following results:

	A	B	C	[
1				
2	2		FUNCTION =IF(A2=2,"1","3"):	1

	A	B	C	
1				
2		4	FUNCTION =IF(A2=2,"1","3"):	3
3				

There are several other similar operators such as less than < (
A2<3 is true when cell A2 is less than 3), LESS THAN or EQUAL
TO <= (a3<=3 is true when cell A3 is no larger than 3), greater than
> (A3>4 is true when A3 is larger than 4), GREATER THAN OR
EQUAL TO >= (A4 >= 4 is true when cell A4 is 4 or larger) and
NOT EQUAL <> (A4<>2 is true when A4 does not contain 2).

Note that the results don't have to be numbers, you can also use
text as the value result, or even a formula.

=IF(A2>=0,SQRT(A2),"Error: Can't square root a negative number")

The above example uses the SQUARE ROOT formula. If the
cell A2 is a positive number it performs a square root, if it's not a
positive number it produces an error message.

We'll describe more logical functions later in the chapter.

There are a number of places we use conditional operators. We
can for example format a cell based on a conditional formula. I'll
describe how to do this later on.

Types of Function

LibreOffice provides a lot of different types of functions. So far
we've concentrated on basic mathematical functions. But LibreOffice
also provides:

- Database Functions
- Date And Time Functions
- Financial
- Information
- Logical

- Mathematical
- Array
- Statistical
- Spreadsheet and
- Text functions.

In addition there is the ability to add functions by programming them – which is beyond the scope of this book but something that you might be interested in learning about later.

Function Wizard

So far we've used the basic formulas available within the NAME BOX, and we've also typed in a few other basic calculations. But LibreOffice Calc has a huge range of formulas to choose from. Almost any mathematical function you're likely to use is available.

And since no one could remember all the formulas that are available there is a Function Wizard that helps you to find and use the formula that you might need.

To open the Function Wizard click on fx in the function toolbar. The Function wizard will open. There is a long list of functions available, so it's important to narrow them down. Click on the Category box to produce a list of Categories for functions that you might use:

Note that when you select one such as Date&Time the function list will contain only functions of that type:

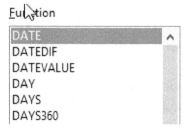

Double clicking on one of the functions will add it to the Formula window:

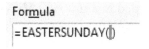

Once you've selected a function you see the name and the current result of the function. If you see an Err it means that there's something wrong with the result. In this case it's because we haven't given the formula any input.

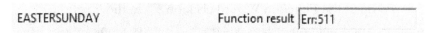

Below the function is a name is a short description of the Function and its' parameters:

And below that is a list of parameters that you can enter:

year f_x ⌷ ⌷

Note that you have the parameter name, then a function

icon , then a text box [   ], and then a shrink

button [ ] .

The simplest thing to do is type whatever the parameter value is in the text box:

You see the result of the parameter you've entered in the function result at the top of the screen:

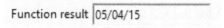

There are two other ways to give the cell a parameter, however.

You can use a reference to a cell first of all. For example, click [ ] and the function wizard shrinks down:

Click on a cell and the parameter that you're entering will reference the cell. For example if I click on the following cell it gets a blue highlight around it:

And the parameter changes to the cell in the function wizard.

When you've selected the cell that you want to reference, you can make the function wizard larger by clicking the Shrink button again .

Finally, we can use the output of a formula as the input value for a parameter by clicking on 𝑓ₓ. You'll then be able to click on another function such as YEAR

Formula   Result │Err:511
=EASTERSUNDAY(YEAR())

And you can keep on nesting the formula in the parameter, for example clicking on

NOW

It's a bit hard to explain it in words but once you try it yourself it's pretty easy to use this functionality to make some quite complicated nested formula:

Formula
=EASTERSUNDAY(YEAR(NOW()))

Which produced the following result at the time I wrote this book:

Function result │05/04/15

One thing to note is that as you're building nested functions it's possible to have a function where you haven't completed all the parameters. You can see the parameters of a function by clicking on the function name in the function window:

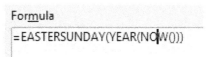

Formula
=EASTERSUNDAY(YEAR(NOW()))

Will show the parameters for the function NOW:

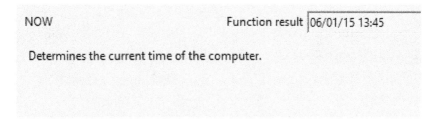

NOW   Function result |06/01/15 13:45

Determines the current time of the computer.

(There aren't any) but if you click on EASTERSUNDAY:

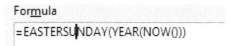

Formula
=EASTERSUNDAY(YEAR(NOW()))

You'll see the parameters that you've entered for that function:

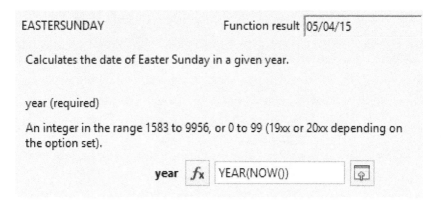

EASTERSUNDAY   Function result |05/04/15

Calculates the date of Easter Sunday in a given year.

year (required)

An integer in the range 1583 to 9956, or 0 to 99 (19xx or 20xx depending on the option set).

year   *fx*   YEAR(NOW())

It's worth trying this out when you're not actually editing an important spreadsheet to get the hang of it. Realistically, the Function Wizard is worth its weight in gold because it's impossible to remember the parameters of every function that you might need to use at some point.

Date And Time Functions

Date and Time are stored in LibreOffice as special types of numbers which are then converted on the fly to read (to a human) like a date. We've already seen how to format a cell to show a date in different formats.

To illustrate, say we take the following cell `1000`, right click on it and `Format Cells...` Select `Date` and then `31/12/1999`. We see the content of the cell change to a date `26/09/1902`.

It's not an obvious feature of LibreOffice Calc (well, except to a computer scientist!) but it means that you can use mathematics with dates.

For example, `=D8+1` would produce the following result:

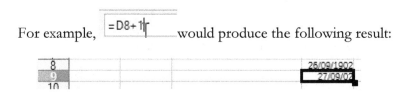

Which is kind of useful when you think about it. LibreOffice does these kind of calculations in the background allowing you to add and subtract days from date fields. Time values are also stored as numbers so you can use similar mathematical operations on them.

You can use this to do other interesting things. For example, to calculate the number of days between two dates:

=DATE(1999,12,10)-DATE(1999,11,1)

(DATE is a function with parameters (YEAR, MONTH, DAY) so this is 10/12/1999 – 1/11/1999.)

Once you understand that date and time functions are actually mathematical in nature it becomes a little easier to see how they combine together.

You can see a list of current DATE and TIME functions at https://help.libreoffice.org/Calc/Date_and_Time_Functions

There are some commonly useful functions however:

DATE (YEAR,MONTH,DAY) – returns a date.

=DATE(2013,1,2) produces the result

02/01/13

DATEVALUE(TEXT) – returns the internal number value for a particular date.

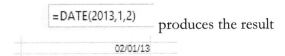 Produces

Function result 41579

.

Note that there are quite a few functions that take the internal integer value of a date. For example, *DAY(NUMBER)* which returns the day number of a particular date.

 produces

Function result 1

So far we've just used DATE values. But LibreOffice Calc can also handle Time values such as:

08:24:00

And Date and Time values such as:

31/12/99 08:32

If you use a formula that is based on just date values such as

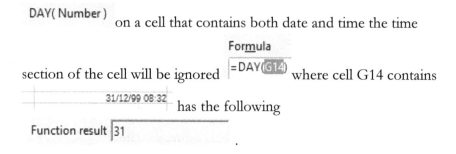

DAY(Number) on a cell that contains both date and time the time section of the cell will be ignored `=DAY(G14)` where cell G14 contains `31/12/99 08:32` has the following Function result `31`.

Similarly, when using a time function on a field containing date and time LibreOffice calc will normally disregard the date. For example with the function HOUR (Number) which takes a internal time number and returns the hour of the day the function `=HOUR(G14)` will show Function result `8`.

The Function Wizard and help documentation is very useful for finding the correct function for the purpose that you need.

Text Functions

So far we've worked with some basic numerical functions and date functions, but we've also worked with text a lot. And just like other basic data types – such as Dates&Time – LibreOffice provides you with a lot of functions that can do things like:

- Change the case of some text
- Convert a number or other data type to text
- Find text strings in text and so on.

To work with text functions open the function wizard by clicking on *fx* and then choose `Text` from the category list.

There are some notable functions available in the list. For example, *TRIM (Text)* takes some text and removes any white space - leading or trailing spaces – from it.

=TRIM(" this is trim") Produces   Function result | this is trim   .

Another interesting function is *UPPER (Text)* which takes some text and makes it upper case. For example

=UPPER(" lOwer case text") produces   Function result | LOWER CASE TEXT

.

The opposite of UPPER is *LOWER (Text)* which works as you'd expect:

=LOWER("UpPER CASE") Produces

Function result | upper case

.

In addition to these functions there are others that can return a number of characters from the left or right of a string. For example *RIGHT (Text, Number)* takes some text and returns the rightmost Number characters from it:

=RIGHT("This is some text",3) Has the

result   Function result | ext   .

You'll often combine these functions together:

=RIGHT(TRIM("This is some text   "),3) Removes the trailing white

space from the text: Function result | ext   .

You can also use text functions to combine text together. For example COCATENATE(Text, Text…) will join several text strings together:

=CONCATENATE("this"," that "," the other") produces

Function result | this that the other   .

You'll sometimes find yourself using COCATENATE with other functions and cell values:

`=CONCATENATE( DAY(c58), " of the month")` which results in

Function result	2 of the month

.

In addition to formulas that convert text, there are several that can change its value. For example *REPLACE (Text, Position, Length, New Text)* which replaces Length number of characters at Position with New Text:

`=REPLACE("This and that",2,3,"hat")` Gives the result

Function result	That and that

.

While I've given an overview of a few text functions there are many more to choose from. You can find out more about the functions available at https://help.libreoffice.org/Calc/Functions_by_Category#Text one section that you may be particularly interested in are the conversion functions which allow you to change text into numbers or other formats.

Mathematical Functions

As you'd expect from a Spreadsheet program, LibreOffice Calc provides a lot of functions. You can see the help files at https://help.libreoffice.org/Calc/Mathematical_Functions but most of these functions work more or less as expected. For example, if you want to do a square root SQRT (number) takes a number and gives you its square root:

`=SQRT(4.5)` results in

Function result	2.1213203436

.

Similarly, if you want to round a number you can use ROUND (Number, Count) which rounds a number to the nearest Count places;

=Round(5.5555,2) produces Function result |5.56 .

There are other functions provided to deal with things like tangents, degrees, Binary operations and so on. For example if you want to generate a random number you could use *RAND()* to return a random number between 0.0 and 1.0 or *RANDBETWEEN(Bottom, Top)* which produces a random number between Bottom and Top:

=RANDBETWEEN(1,100) when I ran it

produced Function result |70 .

It's possible to multiply numbers together with *PRODUCT(Number, Number...)* for example:

=PRODUCT(1,2,3,4,5) has the result Function result |120 .

Most of the commonly used mathematical functions are available.

Logical Functions

We've already covered one of the main Logical Functions, the IF statement. But LibreOffice calc provides all the other standard Logical Functions such as AND, OR, NOT and so on.

For Example AND(Logical Value, Logical Value...) ANDS all the logical values you specify together, so if they are all true it will return true:

=AND(TRUE, FALSE, TRUE) returns Function result |FALSE .

This may seem initially rather useless but if you combine it with the fact you can do conditions such as:

=AND(D2>2,A2<0) which produces Function result |TRUE you

see that it starts to be useful. In this case, if D2 is greater than 2, and A2 is less than 0 it will return TRUE. If either of these conditions is false it will return FALSE.

You can use the Logical functions with the IF function which we've already seen:

=IF(AND(D2>2,A2<0),"In Range", "Out of Range") shows

Function result |In Range

.

OR *(Logical Value, Logical Value…)* returns true when any of its parameters are true:

=OR(A2>0, D2>0) returns Function result |TRUE because while A2 contains -2, D2 is 4 and D2>0 is therefore TRUE.

LibreOffice provides information on all the Logical Functions at https://help.libreoffice.org/Calc/Logical_Functions

Note though that logical functions are most powerful when used together.

Financial Functions

LibreOffice Calc provides a lot of functions that you can use when working on Financial Spreadsheets. For example you can use RATE to calculate the interest rate of an interest payment with a fixed number of payments, or RECEIVED to calculate the amount paid out as a maturity for a fully invested security. YIELD returns the yield on a security that pays a periodic amount of interest.

COUPNUM provides the number of Coupons payable between the settlement and maturity dates.

Most of these Financial Functions work precisely as you'd expect them to. You can find a complete list of them and the parameters that they take at https://help.libreoffice.org/Calc/Financial_Functions_Part_One .

You'll see quite a lot of different functions so I hope you forgive me if I don't try to cover every single one of them!

Statistical Functions

You can use the built-in Statistical Functions to do a wide range of analysis from fairly basic to much more advanced functions. For example, you can use AVERAGE to find the average of a range of cells:

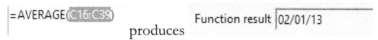 produces

because the range of cells are all dates. Note that with these formulas it's not always obvious that you can include a range of cells into a number parameter as in the above example. It can be worth trying it out and seeing if it produces an error.

You can find the absolute distribution of a sample from the mean using AVEDEV. For example with the following range:

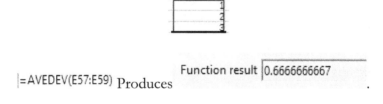

=AVEDEV(E57:E59) Produces .

There are other statistical functions that are useful when working with various types of distribution, averages, to find the distribution covariance. Basically all the standard statistical functions that you might want to use. You can find a list of the ones that you might need at https://help.libreoffice.org/Calc/Statistics_Functions although I find that most of the functions are fairly obvious.

Information Functions

Unlike Statistical, Mathematical and Logical functions which all pretty much work in the way you'd expect from real world experience the Informational Functions are a bit more difficult to understand.

That's because these functions are primarily used to return information about particular cells in the database, or internal information such as errors and whether a cell contains a formula, text or a number.

Say you want to know whether a cell that contains the text FUNCTION =IF(A2=2,"1","3"): is text or not. You can use the informational function ISTEXT(Value) to find out whether the cell is text:

=ISTEXT(C2) produces result Function result TRUE . There are similar functions for numbers (ISNUMBER (Value)) and for many other data types.

One particularly useful informational function is IsBlank (Value) which returns true if the cell doesn't contain anything:

For example when run on the following blank cell the function =ISBLANK(E19) returns Function result TRUE .

There are also formulas that can tell you whether the cell contains an even number ISEVEN_ADD (Value), or whether the cell contains a formula ISFORMULA (Value) and many similar other features that can be very useful in some circumstances.

You can even find out what function a cell contains using FORMULA (Value) for example =FORMULA(D2) returns Function result =IF(A2=2,"1","3") .

I hope that this brief explanations is useful to you. Where most functions provided by LibreOffice Calc carry out operations that you're familiar with – for example, If statements, mathematical or statistical analysis – the information functions provide you with information about the contents of a LibreOffice Spreadsheet.

You can find a comprehensive list of these Information Functions at https://help.libreoffice.org/Calc/Information_Functions .

Array Functions

It can be difficult to explain what an array is, although we've already come close to something very similar. For example when we do a sum on a range of cells:

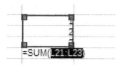

We can think of the range L21:L23 as an Array. And array is a group of cells. It's another word for a Range. In the following example I've selected the range 2Rx3C

Once you think of a Range, an Array makes a lot more sense. But here's the thing… we've already used ranges in functions. The above example using Sum is just one occasion. So, what's the different between a normal function and an Array function? An array function works on each cell in an array separately. For example, if you run SUMPRODUCT it will calculate the product of each cell in the array separately and then add them together.

You can find out more about Array Functions at https://help.libreoffice.org/Calc/Array_Functions .

Note that when you want to return an array you need to click ☐Array on the bottom left hand of the function wizard even when working with array functions.

Database Functions

Most of the Database Functions in LibreOffice Calc deal with ranges of cells. For example DAVERAGE returns the average value of cells in a range which match some search criteria, DCOUNT counts all the items in a range that match a search criteria, DSUM adds all the cells in a range that match some search criteria.

You can find out more about Database functions at https://help.libreoffice.org/Calc/Database_Functions

Spreadsheet Functions

The Spreadsheet functions contain a number of fairly miscellaneous functions such as ones that deal with pivot tables, find out the column or Row of a cell, find out what sheet a cell belongs to, and add hyperlinks to the worksheet.

For example =HYPERLINK("http://www.example.org";"Click here") will display Click Here in a cell and open example.org when you click it.

There are also functions that allow you to choose specific index items in a list, or get a text string back for the name of a particular cell.

These aren't, in the main, functions that are used very often but they're useful when you need them. You can find out the syntax of these functions at https://help.libreoffice.org/Calc/Spreadsheet_Functions .

Next Chapter

In this chapter I've shown you how to use the Function Wizard and I've also described some commonly used functions. Obviously, there are hundreds of functions that you can use within LibreOffice Calc for all kinds of purposes so I haven't specified the parameters of every function that you might use. But I hope that I've taught you enough so you can find the function that you need for any purpose that you might have.

In the next chapter I'm going to describe how to improve the look of your spreadsheet.

!

4 IMPROVING THE LOOK OF THE SPREADSHEET

So far I've shown you some basics about how to enter data, how to do formulas and calculations as well as insert and delete rows. This chapter will show you how to change the appearance of cells, control styles, and insert images.

It's hopefully a bit of a relief after the heavier number crunching we did in the last chapter.

Obviously it's quite nice to be able to make sure that the appearance of your spreadsheet is professional.

Controlling the Appearance of Text

One of the most basic things that you can do is change the appearance of text in particular cells. You can change the Font, Font Size, Text Alignment and colour. This can radically alter the appearance of the document without huge amounts of work.

Most of these options are available from the Text Toolbar:

When using this toolbar make sure that you click into the cell whose text you want to change. If you highlight a particular word you can change the font only for the selection of text that you highlight.

Whereas if you only select a particular cell ALL of the content will be changed.

Changing the Font

Next to the styles and formatting button is the Font Name combo box Liberation Sans. Click on the down arrow to see a list of fonts that you've currently installed on the system:

Note that the first few items are fonts that you've used recently, which are separated by a line from an alphabetical list of all the fonts that you have on your system.

Clicking on a font will change the selection (either the cell or part of the cell) to the font that you've chosen.

Note that next to the font name combo is the font size combo box 10. When you click on the down arrow you'll see a list of standard font sizes:

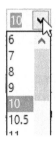

You can also type a specific font size into the box although I don't tend to do that myself personally. I think that the standard font sizes make the document appear to be more consistent.

Bold, Italics and Underline

The next set of options are Bold (or Emphasis) , Italics , and underline . If you select a cell or part of the content of a cell and then click on one of these icons you'll get the appropriate text effect. I.e. click on underline:

Note that it can be difficult to see these effects if the text size is too small. A larger font size can make it easier to see:

00	40.00%
00	60.00%

Changing Text Alignment

Text Alignment controls where you want the text to go. AS A RULE I DON'T RECOMMEND CHANGING TEXT ALIGNMENT. The reason for this is that spreadsheets align text in a standard way, i.e. numbers on one side of the cell and text on the other:

Gross Profit	£600,000

Which makes it instantly easy to see what type the content of a cell is. But you CAN select a cell and then hit 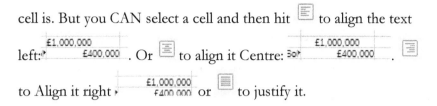 to align the text left: . Or to align it Centre: . to Align it right or to justify it.

Again I don't normally recommend using these functions but they ARE available if you need them.

Changing Text Colour

If you select the down arrow next to the background colour button you can choose a background colour for the cell from the list of colours:

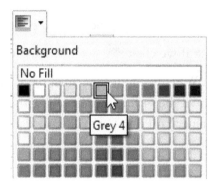

When you click on a colour you'll see the background of the cell change:

Click on the down arrow next to the Font Colour button to show a list of colours for fonts. Click on one to change the font colour.

Number Format

We've already seen how to format a number using the right mouse button. But if you click on **%** the currently selected cell will become a percentage. And if you click on it will become a currency cell. You can still use the right mouse button if you want more control over the exact format of the cell.

Add and Remove Decimal Place from Number

In addition you can reduce by 1 the number of decimal places that LibreOffice shows for a cell by clicking and increase it by clicking on .

Take this cell 1.5555 if we select it and click twice it will show 1.56 but if we click we will see the extra decimal place 1.556 . When we hide a decimal place LibreOffice Calc will round up or down the visible number BUT the number is still stored as the cell value. You don't actually lose data by altering the cell format.

Hiding Grid lines.

By default LibreOffice Calc shows lines around every cell. These are called Grid Lines. If you click on you'll hide these lines.

Tutorial Example Profit and Loss

Total Revenue		£1,000,000	
Costs of Goods Sold		£400,000	40.00%
Gross Profit		£600,000.00	60.00%
Expenses			
Director Salary	£	24,000	
Accounting and Leg'l	£	50,000	1.556
Postal	£	14,000	
Advertising	£	150,000	
Depreciation	£	89,000	
Training	£	45,000	

You'll often use this when you've finished editing a document. Click ⊞ again to turn the grid lines back on.

Indent and Decrease Indent For Cell

You can think of an indent as a little like what happens when you press the Tab key. There is a difference though because when you use tab you add an invisible character to the cell. Indent doesn't actually affect the value you're storing in the cell so it's less liable to cause errors when you export the worksheet to a different format.

To increase the indent select a cell then click ▣ .

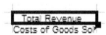

Do decrease the indent select the cell then click ◁ ?

Giving Cells Borders

Sometimes you may want to give a cell or a group of cells a border. The effect of doing this becomes most obvious when you turn off the grid by clicking ⊞ .

First select the cells whose border you want to change:

Then click the down arrow next to cell borders ⊞ ▾ . You'll see a range of graphical options:

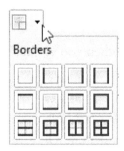

Click on the one that you want to use, for example ☐ .

You'll see the border change around the cells you've selected to match the pattern that you chose.

Inserting Special Characters and Typeset Characters

Sometimes you might want to insert a special character such as a copyright symbol. To do this click on ⌘ Special Character... in the Insert Menu. You'll see the Special Characters dialogue appear. You can choose the Font and the Subset of the font that you're going to insert by clicking on the appropriate combo box.

Font [Liberation Sans ⌄] Subset Of [Basic Latin ⌄]

For example if you select

Font [Wingdings ⌄] then you will see a lot of special symbol characters:

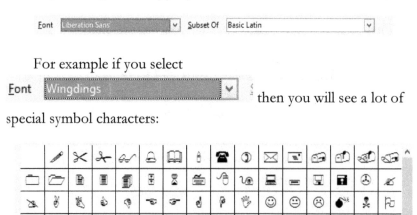

You can scroll down the page to select the character that you want. Note that each Font can have special characters that are unique to it so sometimes it's just a matter of looking until you find the particular special character that you want.

When you see the special character that's ideal for your purpose double click on it to insert it into the cell.

The other set of special characters are typeset characters. For example, hyphens. If you hover your mouse pointer over Formatting Mark you'll see the option to include a Non-breaking space, a Non-breaking hyphen or an Optional Hyphen.

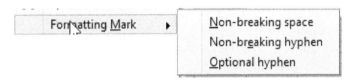

Non-breaking characters (space and hyphen) are used when you want to keep words together when they would otherwise be split over several lines. They're much more commonly used in word processing programs and similar than LibreOffice Calc but they are available if you need them.

Changing Text Case

Sometimes you may want to change the case of the text in a cell or range of cells. First select the text that you want to change. In this case I'm selecting all the values in a cell:

Then hover your mouse over Change Case in the Format menu:

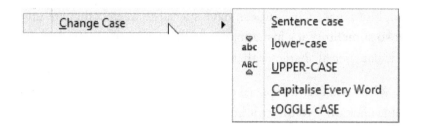

Most of these options are obvious. You can see a preview of what they do. For example toggle case makes every low case letter upper case and vice versa. ThIs to tHIS for example. Upper-case makes every letter upper case This to THIS.

It's not something you use often but it's useful to know about sometimes.

Formatting Characters

We've already dealt with formatting blocks of text above, but there are several more effect that you can get by highlighting the text that you want to change by clicking into the cell, then holding the mouse down at the end of the section and moving the mouse to the beginning:

Then letting go of the mouse and clicking ᴬᴮᶜ Character... in the Format Menu.

The initial page will look very familiar giving you access to changing Font, Font Style and Size which you've learned how to do already. But if in the Tabs you select Font Effects you'll see some extra features that you're not familiar with:

Options

Font colour	Overlining	Overline colour
Automatic ⌄	(Without) ⌄	Automatic ⌄
Effects	Strikethrough	
(Without) ⌄	(Without) ⌄	
Relief	Underlining	Underline colour
(Without) ⌄	(Without) ⌄	Automatic ⌄
☐ Outline	☐ Individual words	
☐ Shadow		

Clicking into one of the effect live Overline will enable you to add various type of Overline Effects

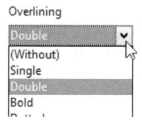

Overlining

Double ⌄
(Without)
Single
Double
Bold

You'll see a preview of this at the bottom of the screen.

<u>____this that or the-other____</u>

Most of these effects are pretty obvious. An Overline goes above the text, strikethrough goes in the middle of the text, and Underline goes under the text. Outline produces a line drawing of the text:

this that or the-other

There are more options available by clicking on the Font Position tab. You can make the text super type (like the th in 9th) or subtype which is below the text. You can also resize the text or alter the spacing between different words.

Formatting Pages

When we're talking about formatting pages we're talking about pages that could be printed out. So, when we click on

Page... in the Format menu LibreOffice opens the Page Style window at the default page tab which allows you to change the format of the print out LibreOffice generates when you choose to print.

Some of the changes you make with this option won't be visible until you run a print preview. So, before worrying that your changes haven't had an effect press to make sure that you see how the document will really be printed.

The first option you see is the Paper Format option which allows you to choose a standard size like A4 or a custom paper size using width and height.

Paper format

Format: A4

Width: 21.00cm

Height: 29.70cm

The default margins vary depending on paper format, but you can also change them manually. Think of the margins as the white space at the top, left and right hand side of the paper. It's used so that you can handle the paper without smudging the writing, or write notes on the edge of the paper.

Margins

Left: 2.00cm

Right: 2.00cm

Top: 2.00cm

Bottom: 2.00cm

You can also choose whether to print in "Book" format with Right and Left pages, or only right or only left or mirrored.

The Format option controls how LibreOffice Calc numbers each page. The standard format is page 1, 2, 3 etc. but there are other Formats to choose from. These often show up when you want to change the header or footer.

Format: 1, 2, 3, ...

Changing Page Borders

You can switch onto the borders tab by clicking Borders .

The most common way of choosing the line arrangements around the page is using first command you see. Click on the one that has the format that you want. Probably the most common is which surrounds the entire page with a border.

Line arrangement

Default

You can also choose the style of the line around the page, and the width etc. of the line. These options are quite self-explanatory.

Background Colour or Background Image

While this is an option it's not one that I think many people use. But you can add a background colour to the page by clicking onto the Background tab. Make sure the as box is set as following  and choose a colour.

Using a background Image – which can be thought of as a watermark – is probably more common. Set the As box by clicking on it to Graphic

Click on  to show a Find Graphics dialogue which works like an Open dialogue. Chose the picture that you want, and you'll see it appear in the preview window.

Note that you can choose the position by clicking on ⊙ Position and then one of the options on the position options box on the right:

In the above case it will position the image right in the centre. The image will only be displayed once. You can make the image stretch to cover the entire worksheet by selecting ⦿ Area or make it repeat itself so it covers the entire document by selecting ⦿ Tile .

When you add a graphic to the page you won't see it when you're editing. But if you do a print preview 🖼 you'll see it appear then.

Inserting a Header or a Footer

A header is the text at the top of the printed page. You can change is by clicking on Header. A footer is at the bottom of the page, click Footer to edit it.

You'll see a lot of options that allow you to change the size and position of the header or footer. There is also a

More...

button that allows you to change its colour, and a

Edit...

button that allows you to change the text. Probably the main thing that you will do his hit the Edit button. This opens the Header or Footer dialogue.

When you do this you'll see a combination of three boxes one of which has the name of the spreadsheet by default.

Left area	Centre area	Right area
	Profit and Loss	

The left area box contains text that will appear in the left hand side of the header or footer. The Centre area contains the text that will appear in the middle, and the right area… well, you get the idea.

Type text into any of these three boxes to make the text appear in the header or footer.

Below these boxes are some automatically generated fields.

If you click on one of these buttons you'll see a text field appear that corresponds to the button name (hover the mouse over a button to see the name of the command)

Clicking on the above button will therefore add the Date to the area of the header or footer you're entering text into:

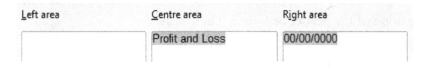

Left area	Centre area	Right area
	Profit and Loss	00/00/0000

One exception is the text attribute button which allows you to change the appearance of the text.

Sheet Options

In the Page formatting dialogue you can choose sheet options by clicking on the Sheet tab. Note that Sheet Options control how worksheets are printed or displayed.

The First set of options allows you to change the first page number (i.e. make the sheet start from page 0 or 8 or whatever) and which order sheets are printed in (left to right or top to bottom) with a handy preview that shows you how the sheets will be printed.

The next item determines what you're going to print. For example you can choose to print column and row headers, or Formulae.

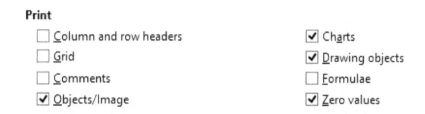

Finally you can choose not to scale the worksheet to reduce paper consumption. This option is most useful when you find the worksheet is difficult to read when you print it out.

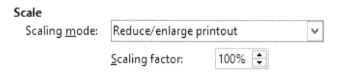

Modifying Styles

So far in this chapter I've shown you ways to change the appearance of cells on an individual basis, and in an earlier tutorial I showed you how to change them based on styles. But what I didn't show you was how to change or add new styles to the worksheet.

For example, say you wanted to create a new Percent style that you use when displaying percent.

To make such a style first format the cell how you want to, using any of the options (i.e. font size, colour etc.) that we've already discussed.

I might choose to change the font, increase its size, and add bold:

Make sure that the styles and formatting dockable window is on the left hand side of the screen. If necessary click on 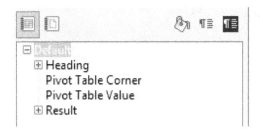 in the toolbar to toggle it on.

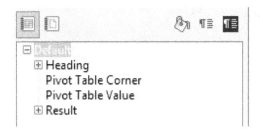

Click on the New Style from Selection  and type in a name:

Press enter. You'll see the new style appear in the style and formatting window.

You can modify a style by clicking onto a cell of that style,
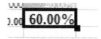
which will result on the style name being highlighted in
the style and formatting window (see example above for Percentage),
changing the formatting for the cell for example by making it larger:

And then clicking the update style icon ▊▊. All the other cells
with that style will change to match the new choices you've made.

Images and Movies

One of the most common ways to improve a document is to
include images in it. We've already seen the ability to include
watermarks in a document but it's possible to add pictures and gifs to
a worksheet and the move them around in order to improve the
document. For example, including company logos or pictures of
chairman addressing his loyal supporters – ok, maybe not the latter
but it's pretty obvious what you can use these functions for.

In the same way that you can insert an image you can also insert
a movie which someone looking at the spreadsheet through a screen
or projector can play.

Inserting an Image

Hover your mouse over Image in the Insert menu and click
From File.

You'll see an Insert Image dialogue which works like a File Open
dialogue. Go to the correct directory

« Google Drive ▸ Tom ▸ NEA

And then double click on the image you want to insert. You'll see the image appear in the worksheet.

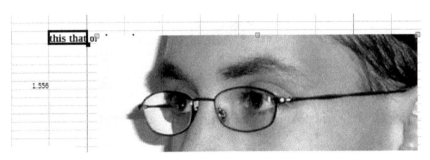

Sound or Movie

Click on 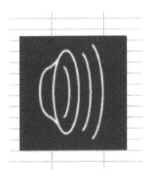 Movie and Sound... and you'll see an Insert Movie and Sound dialogue which works the same way as an Open File dialogue. Double click on the sound or movie that you want to play. You'll see the Movie or Sound appear in the worksheet like an Image:

For example if you insert a sound you'll see the following image appear:

When you click onto it you'll see that at the bottom of the page you see the Play Movie or Sound toolbar.

These options work as you'd expect. For example, click on to play the sound, or use the slider to move forwards and backwards in the sound.

Note that Movies, Images and Sound are all objects. You can carry out some operations on them such as moving them around in the worksheet in the same way.

Moving an object

To move an object click and hold on the object then drag it to wherever in the worksheet you want it to appear. Note that while you're moving it a "shadow" will show you exactly where you're moving it to. When you let go the object will move to wherever you put the mouse.

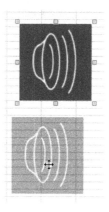

Resizing an object

Click on an object to select it and you'll see a border with green squares appear. Click and hold on one of the green rectangles and move the mouse towards the centre of the image to make it smaller, and away to make it larger.

If you make it larger you might find that the image becomes pixilated – or in other words blocky – because the computer program doesn't have any more information to display the image. It shows the same amount of information over a larger area.

Note that if you use the rectangles in the corner you move both sides, if you use the rectangle in the middle of an image you move only the side that the image is on.

Anchoring an object

You can think of an anchor for an object like a reference point that the object will remain the same distance from. So, in other words, when the anchor moves so will the object. You can move the position of the object relative to the anchor manually but when the reference point moves so will the object.

By default LibreOffice anchors an object on the page. This means that it stays at the same place in the page even if you insert or delete cells above or below it.

If you want to change this to anchor to a particular cell first select the cell, then right click on the object and hover your mouse over Anchor then select To Cell

Now the image is anchored to the cell you selected. If you were

to insert a row below the cell so that your anchor cell doesn't move the image will remain in the same place. If you insert a row above the cell the object will move with the anchor cell.

In other words, LibreOffice Calc will retain the position of the image relative to the anchor cell automatically when you move the cell.

Grouping objects

You can sometimes get to the point that you have a lot of object in your document and you want to combine them together so that they don't end up getting split up. You can group objects together (so LibreOffice treats them as all the same object).

TO group images together select both images. You do this by clicking on one image, then hold the shift key down and clicking on the second image. Note both objects will get a blue border around them.

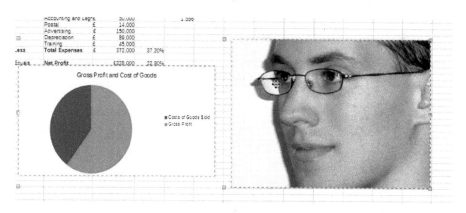

Keep on holding the shift key and clicking until you've selected all the objects that you want to include in the group. Let go of the shift key when you've finished selecting all the images or objects you want to group together. Then right click on one of the objects and hover your mouse over Group. Click on it.

You'll now be able to resize, move and so on the group as if it were a single object. If you right click on the Group and then select Ungroup LibreOffice will treat the objects as separate items again. If you use Edit Group you'll be able to change individual objects in the group but the group itself will remain.

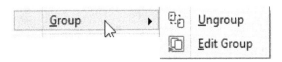

When you've finished editing the group you would right click on an object in the group, and then select Exit Group:

Merging Cells

Merging cells means combing them together into one cell. For example, if you have the following two cells:

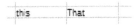

Select them both, then go to Merge Cells:

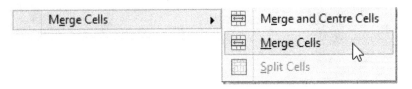

You will see a message that asks if you want to add the content of the second to the first cell. Click Yes if you want to keep it, or no if you don't.

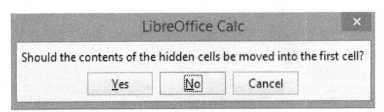

Note that when you merge a cell the one that "disappears" remains part of the spreadsheet, it's just hidden as below:

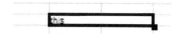

You're not actually deleting it you're just hiding it. The value in the cell will remain. If you were to right click on the cell and select

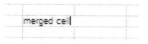 the old cell would reappear including the value even if we change the value in the merged cell:

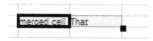

When we click on split cells becomes:

Merging a cell is most often used cosmetically to make the appearance of a spreadsheet look better, for example by making a large "title" cell.

Changing the Appearance of Cells Based on their Content

There are a lot of options to control the appearance of a cell based on its content. Select the cell or range of cells where you want to apply the conditional formatting and then select the option that you want.

I tend to find that it's best to just set a condition for the cell and

not try to use the other functions. When you select the condition you'll be able to specify whether your condition is true for all cells, just checks against the value of each cell, uses a Logical Formula or is based on the date.

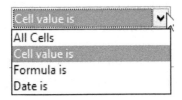

I tend to select Cell Value is most often, since this is checking against the value of each cell in the range that you've selected. Then you can choose the basic comparison. For example, Equal to, less than etc.:

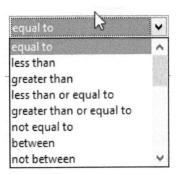

And add the value into the final box. For example, the formatting you select will apply in this case if the value is less than or equal to 4.

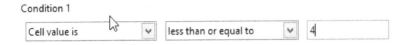

The final step is to select what style will apply to the cell if the condition is matched.

Apply Style

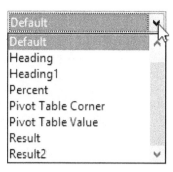

Note that you can have more than one condition for the cell if you click **Add** . Where two conditions are matched the last style will be the one that is applied to the cell.

Condition 1	Cell value is <= 4		
Condition 2			
Cell value is	greater than		0
Apply Style	Default		3

You can edit a condition by clicking on it. You can also remove the condition you're currently editing by clicking on **Remove** . You can find out some more details about some of the advanced features like colour scales on https://help.libreoffice.org/Calc/Conditional_Formatting .

Themes

Themes are a facility that LibreOffice Calc has that changes the appearance of a worksheet to match some predesigned look. To use themes you'll have to use the View menu to add a new toolbar. LibreOffice Calc has a lot of toolbars that can allow you to do all sorts of things. Many, like the Tools and the Draw toolbar are hidden because they're not frequently used. But when you need them knowing that they are there comes in handy!

In the View menu hover your mouse over toolbars. You'll see a list of toolbars that you can use in the program. Many of them you'll already have seen. If you click on  you'll see a new toolbar.

This is the Tools Toolbar:

One of the options in the Tools toolbar is themes . Click on it. You'll see the

Themes dialogue,

Double click on one of the options to use one of the predefined themes. Some of them are quite subtle, but others are quite garish or obvious. You'll have to try them out to see if there are ones that you like. For example, PC Nostalgia will make your spreadsheet look very old fashioned:

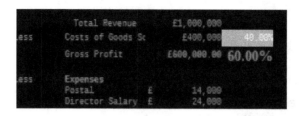

Warning: when you change the theme of a spreadsheet, LibreOffice Calc doesn't offer an undo facility.

Draw Toolbar

Sometimes you may want to add squares, rectangles or other shapes to a spreadsheet. While I don't do it often there are two main ways to get shapes that you want into the document. The first is to insert an image. The problem with this is that it will go on top of your spreadsheet hiding any of the cells beneath the image.

But LibreOffice offers a solution. The draw toolbar. In the View menu hover your mouse over toolbars. Click on  to show the Draw Toolbar at the bottom of the screen.

Most of these options are obvious. For example if you want to draw a rectangle click on

Then go to the place on the image where you want to draw the shape, click and hold the mouse button and move to the opposite corner.

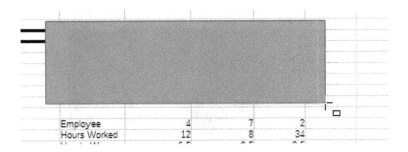

But we've still got a shape that goes "on top" of the cells beneath. You can select an object by clicking on ⌕ and then change the background colour to None in order to make it see through.

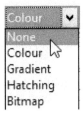

Note that the image is still on top of your cells.

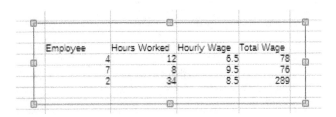

An alternative is to right click on the shape then hover your mouse over arrange and click ☰ To Background which will sent the image to the background, i.e. behind the cells.

Employee	Hours Worked	Hourly Wage	Total Wage
4	12	6.5	78
7	8	9.5	76
2	34	8.5	289

Note that if you choose this option the cell lines will show up while you're editing the worksheet, but are generally invisible when you go to print it out.

There are a lot of other shapes to choose from including 3d shapes, lines, and text. In general these functions work the way that you would expect but it's worth trying them out to see if they improve the look of your spreadsheet.

Next Chapter

In this chapter I've described a lot of ways to improve the look of the spreadsheet.

In the next chapter I'll describe more about how to analyze Data.

5 DATA, CHARTS AND OTHER FUNCTIONS

More on Charts

We've already covered the basic steps to creating charts earlier in the book, but in this section we're going to go into a little more detail. First, highlight the cells that you want to include in the table. For example with the following table:

Employee	Hours Worked	Hourly Wage	Total Wage
4	12	6.5	78
7	8	9.5	76
2	34	8.5	289

We might want a graph of employee vs Total Wage. You select ranges that aren't adjacent by selecting the first column as normal, then adding to the selection by holding down the ctrl button on the keyboard at the same time as you use the left mouse button and the mouse to select extra cells.

Employee	Hours Worked	Hourly Wage	Total Wage
4	12	6.5	78
7	8	9.5	76
2	34	8.5	289

Once you're happy with your selection press the Chart

button located in the toolbar.

You'll see the Chart Wizard.

The first task is to choose the type of chart that you want. In this case, I'm going to go for a column chart.

Looking at the graphic you can see what the type of chart looks like. Many of these chart types you'll have come across on a fairly regular basis although some – like Net charts – are not used nearly so frequently.

Some of the options in the Chart wizard are simply aesthetic. You can for example choose to give the chart a 3-D effect.

☐ 3-D Look Realistic ⌄   And if you choose a 3d effect you can also choose what kind of 3d shape the chart should take on. For example you can choose a cylinder shape.

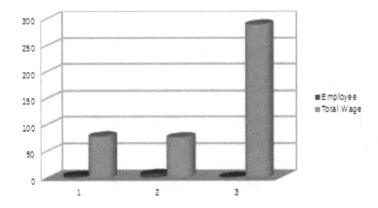

When looking at the above chart preview you can see that it's subtly wrong – don't worry, using the wrong series is fairly common event and I'll show you how to fix it later! What we're doing at this stage is simply choosing the chart and appearance.

Click [Next >>] to go onto the next task.

Data Range

The first option is the Data range option. Note that this can look intimidating:

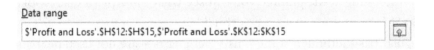

Data range

$'Profit and Loss'.$H$12:$H$15,$'Profit and Loss'.$K$12:$K$15

The first section is the worksheet name followed by a dot and the range. Notice that the $ symbols are part of the format for the cell range which is H12:H15 in this case. After you've defined this range there is a comma and the second range.

While you can define this range by typing it in the proper format if you shrink the dialogue using [ ] you can change the range with the mouse in the normal way.

The next option is to choose whether to use data series in columns or rows.

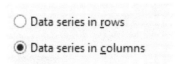

In our case we're using data in columns. An example of data in rows could be

Employee	4	7	2
Hours Worked	12	8	34
Hourly Wage	6.5	9.5	8.5
Total Wage	78	76	289

Note that we can see the preview in the spreadsheet already. And it doesn't look right as I've already explained. The Employee should be a label on the graph and we've included it as a different data series:

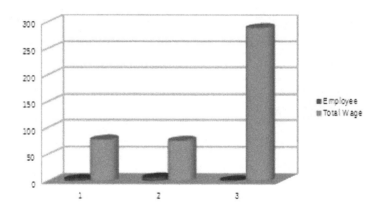

You can change it so the first column is a label and not a data series by clicking on ☐ First column as label which immediately makes things better:

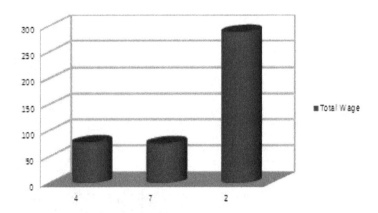

In the row example I used a different set of choices, specifying the data series was in rows and the column and row were labels

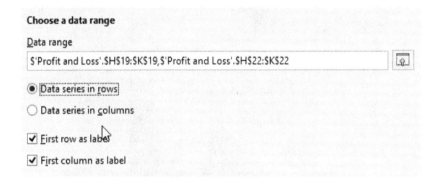

To produce the following preview:

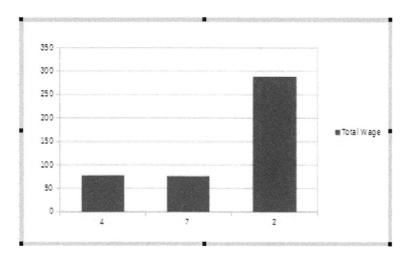

I find that sometimes you just have to fiddle with the options to get the chart to work exactly as you want it. It's generally possible to change your mind with some of these options so don't worry if you're not quite sure what an option does – give it a try and change it back if you're not happy.

But once you are happy click on Next >> .

The next series of options allows you to change the range for particular data series. I very rarely use any of these options since you generally select the correct cells for each data series at an earlier stage. So click Next >> .

The final task allows you to choose the labels for your chart. When you've done that click on Finish .

I find that charts are one of the most useful features of a spreadsheet program. They allow you to visualize data so much more easily than any other method.

Names

We've already used Names before when we referenced

something like cell C12. A name is a cell reference that we've customised so that it is a combination of meaningful words.

Automatically Creating

You can automatically name cell ranges by firstly selecting the range of cells that you want to name.

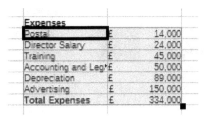

And then hover your mouse over Names in the Insert menu and click on Create.

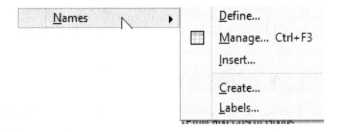

Choose where to determine the names from:

Note that when you click onto one of the cells in the range which you've given a name, such as Director Salary the name box shows something interesting:

When you start to type the name into a new cell, you see an auto complete suggestion that includes it:

And you can do sums with it the same way as if it was just an ordinary cell reference:

Defining Name manually

While it's often quicker to define a name automatically it is possible to define one manually as well. Select the Cell or Range that you want to name. Then hover your mouse over Names in the Insert menu and then click Define:

Type in the name that you want to give the cell(s)

The next set of options show you the range that you're giving the name to. You can change this manually but it's generally better to use the mouse to select the range before you begin.

Finally, you can choose to change the Scope of the Name. The Scope of the Name is where in your document you can use it.

So, if you select Document (Global) you can access it throughout the entire file.

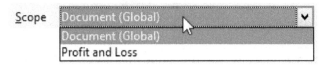

The other option is the worksheet. If you choose this option the name will only be available in the current worksheet. If you move to another worksheet in the worksheet tabs you won't be able to access the name.

There are also some range options to allow you to print the range, and filter or sort it.

Data Ranges
In the same way that you can name individual cells or ranges above you can also define Data ranges. This is particularly useful when you're doing multiple operations on a particular range. Instead of having to select them every time you can define a range once and use it multiple times.

Defining Ranges
The first step to defining a Data Range is to select it in your worksheet (remember that you can use the ctrl key to select ranges in different areas of the worksheet):

Expenses		
Postal	£	14,000
Director Salary	£	24,000
Training	£	45,000
Accounting and Leg'	£	50,000
Depreciation	£	89,000
Advertising	£	150,000
Total Expenses	£	334,000

Then in the Data menu click on Define Range

Type in your name. It should be something that you'll be able to remember later on – so use something meaningful.

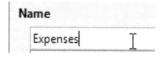

Click on 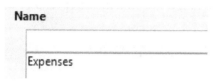 to give you advanced options to do things like keep formatting, or specify that the range includes column labels.

Click [Add] and the new Data Range will appear in the list.

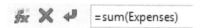

Click OK. Once you've added a Data range you can use it as if it were a specified range in formulas and anywhere else you can use a Cell Range in LibreOffice Calc.

f_x ✗ ↵ =sum(Expenses)

Selecting Range

Sometimes you may want to select a range that you've defined in the earlier step. Although you can obviously use the mouse LibreOffice also allows you to select the Data Range via its name. You do this by clicking on Select Range... in the Data menu. This displays the Select Data Range dialogue which shows a list of all the currently defined global ranges in your spreadsheet or the current worksheet.

Double click on the name of the range that you want to select.

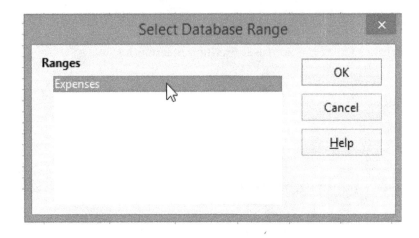

You'll see the range selected in the spreadsheet:

Less	Expenses			
	Postal	£	14,000	
	Director Salary	£	24,000	
	Training	£	45,000	
	Accounting and Leg'l	£	50,000	
	Depreciation	£	89,000	
	Advertising	£	150,000	
Less	Total Expenses	£	334,000	33.40%

Comments

Sometimes you may want to include comments about a particular cell in the worksheet. This can include things like how the cell is calculated, or a description about specific terms. Click onto the cell which you want to comment on, then in the Insert menu click on ☐ Comment Ctrl+Alt+C .

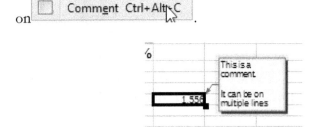

When you click off the comment it will disappear. But note that the cell has a little red square at the right hand corner.

1.556

Clicking on the cell will display the comment again.

Insert a Sheet from File

Sometimes you may want to insert worksheets from a file. In the Insert Menu click on to bring up the Insert Sheet From File dialogue. You'll be inserting a text file most often. The first step is that LibreOffice opens an Insert File dialogue where you select the file to insert. Then it will bring up a dialogue that allows you to specify the format of the worksheet.

Because each worksheet will be different probably the best thing to do is experiment with the options and check the help at https://help.libreoffice.org/scalc/modules/scalc/ui/textimportcsv/charset?Language=en-GB&System=WIN&Version=4.2#bm_id315790911

One thing that you need to pay a lot of attention to is the format of the file. For example, if it's separated by commas or tabs. While LibreOffice will try to work it out for you it's important to keep checking the preview to make sure that the choices that you make will produce the correct results.

Version Control

LibreOffice Calc provides a limited type of Version Control. While if you want the most powerful version control I'd still suggest that you use an external software solution. But by clicking on Versions... in the File Menu you can bring up an option that allows you to store the website as it currently is. Just click on Save New Version and you'll have an option to write who saved it, and be able to see the version in the version list.

Existing versions

Date and time	Saved by	Comments
10/01/2015 13:17		
10/01/2015 13:21		Thomas Ecclestone

You can compare the current version with an old version by clicking on the old version and then Compare. Double click on an old version to open it. But note that you'll only be able to reopen it in read-only format. You'd have to save it as some other file name before you can edit the old version.

You can return to the most recently saved version by clicking on Reload in the File Menu. But note that if you do this you'll permanently lose any changes since the last time you saved the version.

Track Changes

In addition to version control you also have the ability to record the changes that you have made to the spreadsheet via functionality called Track Changes. This is useful when more than one person is editing a spread sheet. The person who owns the document can decide whether to accept changes that someone else has made to it.

Hover your mouse over Changes in the Edit menu and click on record

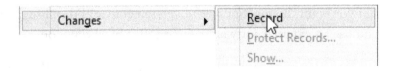

This will start to record the changes that you've made.

If you want to prevent someone else accepting or rejecting changes you can click on Protect Records... and then type in a password that prevents anyone turning off recording or accepting or rejecting changes without the password that you supplied.

Make as many changes as you want. When you change something you'll see a visual indication that you've made the change. For example, a red border.

You can hide some changes if you click on Show (which is below Protect Records) Sho̲w....

If you want to accept or reject changes and you've added a password you'll have to click on ✔ Protect Records... and enter the password.

Once you've done this click on, or if the changes aren't protected, click on Accept or Reject... which you can get to by hovering your mouse over Changes in the Edit menu. You'll see the accept or reject changes dialogue. Select one of the changes in the list

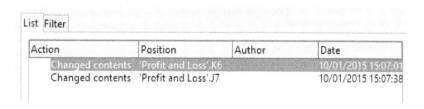

List	Filter		
Action	Position	Author	Date
Changed contents	'Profit and Loss'.K6		10/01/2015 15:07:01
Changed contents	'Profit and Loss'.J7		10/01/2015 15:07:38

And then click on Accept if you want to keep the changes, or click on Reject if you don't want to keep the changes.

Fill

While we've already come across the fill command I think that it might be useful to go in a little more depth. Filling is the act of using the content of a cell or a range of cells to populate other cells. For example, you can use filling complete a series.

First select the numbers in the series

Then move the mouse over to the small square at the end of the series, click and hold, then drag the square to the end of the series:

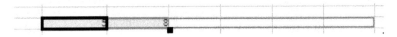

The outline of the series is in purple. The series is completed automatically.

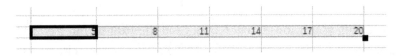

You can have more control over the fill in the Edit menu, especially using the series option when you've got a complex series to fill, i.e. where you want to adjust the increment. You can also fill dates and formula.

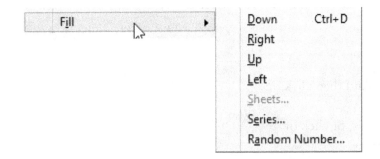

Data Operations

LibreOffice offers a lot of Data operations that allow you to sort data, filter it, and work out subtotals. We've seen some of these functions (in effect) already when we used functions to get results like sums and averages. But the Data Menu offers a lot more Data Operators that can be very useful sometimes.

A lot of these operators work on ranges of cells so it's important to make sure that when you use them you select the right range. For example you'll often not want to include subtotals in the range if you're producing an average.

Another thing to think about is making sure that you keep a backup of the file before using some of these operations in case you make a mistake. This can happen when you're sorting, validating or running statistical analysis on data but it's probably good practice whatever else you're doing with the spreadsheet.

Some of these options don't have undo functions. So regular saving, making sure that you keep the current file safe so that you don't lose your work is a very good idea.

Grouping

You use Grouping so you can hide parts of a worksheet while you're working on them. Sometimes it can be hard to see the wood for the trees. The first step with grouping is to select the cells that you want to group.

Then hover your mouse over Group and Outlines in the Data menu and click on Group... F12 .

Normally you'll choose to include Rows. But you can hide the columns as well, although this is often problematic because it can hide more information than you want.

When you group Rows together you'll see a little minus sign next to the row headers for the group.

		Expenses			
8	Less	Expenses			
9		Postal	£	14,000	
10		Director Salary	£	24,000	
11		Training	£	45,000	
12		Accounting and Leg-£		50,000	
13		Depreciation	£	89,000	
14		Advertising	£	150,000	
15	Less	Total Expenses	£	372,000	37.20%
16					

Click on the ![-] and you'll see the Group collapse (i.e. it will be hidden).

		Expenses			
8	Less	Expenses			
15	Less	Total Expenses	£	372,000	37.20%
16					
17	Equals	Net Profit		£228,000	22.80%
18					

Don't worry that you've lost the data. All you have to do to show the group again is to click on ![+].

Note that clicking into any cell in the group and then selecting ![icon] Ungroup... Ctrl+F12 from the Data->Groups and Outline menu will remove the group and return the cells to "normal".

Sorting Data

Say you wanted to sort the following data:

Expenses		
Postal	£	14,000
Director Salary	£	24,000
Training	£	2,400
Accounting and Leg-£		50,000
Depreciation	£	189,000
Advertising	£	150,000

The first step is to highlight all the cells, and then click on

 in the Data Menu.

When you look at the Sort Dialogue you see immediately a section saying what you're sorting it by. In this case, you're not sorting by the right thing – we want to sort by columns, not rows.

Sort key 1

In your case, you may be sorting by the right thing (i.e. columns or rows) but if you want to sort by row when your sort key says columns or vice versa click on Options in the tab window.

These options allow you to choose if the sort is case sensitive (i.e. treats "A" as identical to "a"), contains range labels (which in this case we want to don't want to select but which is useful if we've got headers for the columns or rows in the range)

Finally, because we're sorting the rows we click ⦿ Top to bottom (sort rows) .

Once we've chosen our options we go back to the Sort Criteria tab.

Click on the Sort Key to choose which column or row to sort the range on.

Sort key 1

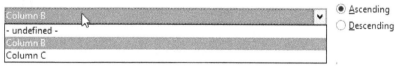

In this case it's Column C.

Then choose whether you want to sort ascending or descending.

Click 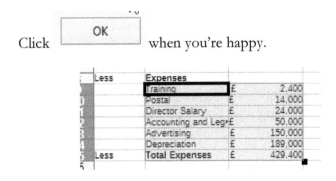 when you're happy.

Often it's good to experiment with these settings since it can be hard to get the exact result that you want. I generally suggest making sure you save the file before you run a sort in case you make any mistakes.

Filtering Data with the Standard Filter

You use filtering to hide and sort data. The first step to using Filters is to select the range of cells that you're going to filter, and then go to the Data Menu and Standard Filter.

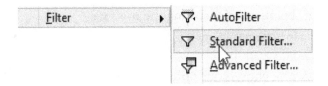

This will bring up the Standard Filter Dialogue. You must choose the Field that you want to Filter. In this case Column C

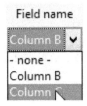

Then select one of the Conditions. Most of these Conditions are pretty self-explanatory. For example Filtering by a >= means filtering by greater than or equal to. < is less than. Just like in the IF Function.

Condition

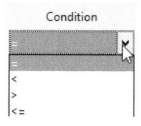

Our first Filter condition is done. But what happens if you want more than one filter condition?

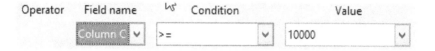

Well, we need to decide if we want to AND the next condition or use OR as the operator. If we use AND, both conditions must be true. If we use OR, if either condition is true the value will be displayed.

Operator

Then, once we've selected the operator we can click ⊞ Options to access advanced options to sort based on case, use regular expressions (which is a little advanced for this book) or remove duplicates. When we're happy with it click OK.

Note that results that don't match our filter have been removed:

If you want to remove the filter click into the group that contains the filter, and then select  Reset Filter from the Filters options in the Data Menu.

Filtering Data with the Auto-Filter

First, select the range of data that you want to auto filter. Then click on Filter>AutoFilter in the Data menu.

This will bring up the AutoFilter dialogue. You may see a message asking if you want the first line to be used as headers. I tend to suggest using No, unless the first line really are headers.

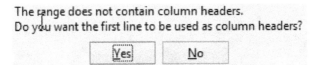

You'll see little down arrows by the items that LibreOffice has detected ought to be filtered.

When you click on the arrow you'll see the autofilter dialogue. This dialogue includes a list of all the values in the field, where clicking on the ✔ will hide the value and clicking on ✔ All will select all of the values to hide.

You can also choose to sort ascending or descending the value, noting that when you're sorting multiple values you're going to sort an entire line at a time based on the filter.

Sort Ascending

Sort Descending

The other options are pretty obvious. You can filter a series of numbers based on the values that are the largest 10 numbers by clicking on Top 10 , or by cells that are Empty by clicking on Empty or not empty with Not Empty . You can show only one item my clicking on it in the list and then clicking [icon] or you can hide the current item and show everything else by selecting an item on the list and then clicking [icon] .

If you click on Standard Filter... you'll see the standard filter dialogue I described above.

Pivot Tables
LibreOffice calc supports the use of Pivot Tables. This is quite an advanced feature that many people have problems with. The best

way to find out how to use it is to refer to https://wiki.documentfoundation.org/images/4/49/CG3408-PivotTables.pdf which provides quite a detailed explanation of this useful functionality.

Statistics

LibreOffice does provide some statistical analysis capability through the Statistics options in the Data Menu:

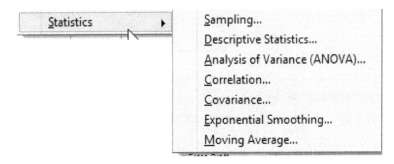

As you can see it's possible to do Sampling, Variance analysis and so on. However, I'd say that in general it's better to look for a dedicated tool such as http://projects.gnome.org/gnumeric/ or you could use the Deducer or Rstudio interfaces to R.

Ggobi might also be worth checking out as a decent tool for data visualization.

Subtotals

For completeness I should mention that you can automatically run subtotals such as products, sums or counts using Subtotals... in the Data window. Highlight the cells that you want to run totals on and you'll see the dialogue.

The first line gives you the option of what to group by. For example, employee number. Then you can choose which fields to run the subtotal on

Calculate subtotals for

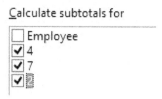

And what type of subtotal to use:

Use function

Sum
Count
Average
Max
Min
Product

I've only given a short overview here. You can find out more in the help https://help.libreoffice.org/Calc/Subtotals but I honestly don't use the automatic subtotal function often. I much prefer to create the formulas manually because that way you have fine control over how results are calculated.

Validity

Sometimes you may want to have a way of making sure that the data that you are entering into a form is basically correct. Or, indeed, give someone a message about what the correct information is for the form.

LibreOffice Calc provides a Validity option to provide some basic checks when you're inputting data.

Select the cell or range of cells where you want to apply validity checking rules and then click on Validity... in the Data Menu to bring up the Validity dialogue.

The first set of options allow you to control what type of data is entered into the cell. For example, you can restrict it to a date, time, or particular types of numbers.

Allow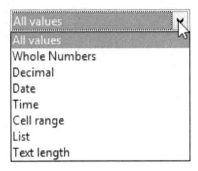

Once you've selected the data type you can choose whether to allow the cell to be blank. ☑ Allow blank cells and then you can choose to put in some data rules. For example, if you choose a Whole Number you can set a valid range, or require it to be greater than a value etc.

Click on the Input Help tab to give people suggestions about what the cell contains. By default this doesn't give you help when you select the cell. If you toggle it on by clicking on the rectangle ☑ Show input help when cell is selected every time you select the cell it will display an information dialogue with the Title and Content that you enter into the form.

Controlling the Validity Error Alert

When someone tries to enter a value into the form that LibreOffice decides isn't valid there will be an Error Message. But sometimes you may want to control the text and the seriousness of one of these errors. You can do this from the Error Alert tab.

One of the most important things in this tab is the Action box. This says what will happen when the error is generated. The default option, stop, prevents someone putting data that doesn't validate into the field.

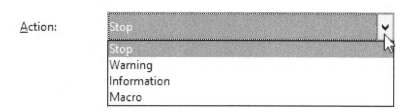

Warning allows you to give someone the option to override the error, whereas information just informs them that they've made an error.

Macro automatically runs a piece of code that you've written. Macros can do almost anything that LibreOffice Calc can do. You click on Browse... to select the macro that you want to use. Macros are a little bit advanced for this manual but it's worth investigating them if you're a power user that wants to customise the functionality of LibreOffice very extensively.

Once you've chosen whether to stop, give a warning etc. the next two field Title (which is the title of the dialogue) and Error Message (which is the text within the dialogue) are pretty easy to understand. They are the error message that you want displayed.

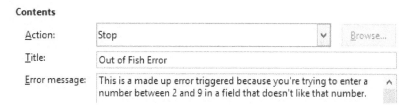

Will produce this error message when you enter the wrong number:

The above error message is slightly misleading because we specified the field was a whole number. So if you try to enter a date or a decimal number it'll also produce an error. When describing the error you've got to include all the possible circumstances that might cause the error to be triggered.

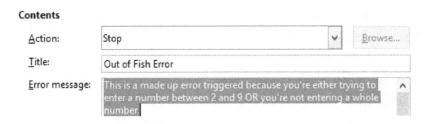

Consolidate

Say you have three worksheets. A totals worksheet, and a July and August worksheet.

The First step is to define the ranges that you're going to use. In the July worksheet select the squares:

	A	B	C	D	E
1	July				
2		Product	Retail Price	Sales	Total
3		Product 1	£100	100	10000
4		Product 2	£50	23	1150
5		Product 3	£400	78	31200
6		Product 4	£2000	2	4000
7					
8					

And in the Name box type in the name that you want to give those squares:

Repeat the process in August. Now, in the totals worksheet click in to the cell where you want the result to be printed.

In the Data Menu click on Consolidate… .

First set the Function. In this case we're going to use Average.

There are a lot of functions to choose from such as Average, Sum, and Product and so on. They work pretty much as you'd expect. Our next step is to select data ranges. When you click down on the Source Data Ranges box you'll see a list which you may have to scroll down until you see the ranges that you've defined in an earlier step.

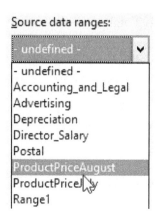

Click on the range to select it. Note that the source data range box displays the range you've selected:

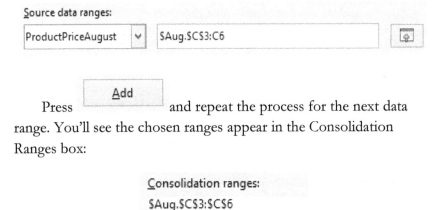

Source data ranges:

ProductPriceAugust   ⌄ $Aug.$C$3:C6

Press **Add** and repeat the process for the next data range. You'll see the chosen ranges appear in the Consolidation Ranges box:

Consolidation ranges:
$Aug.$C$3:$C$6
$July.$C$3:$C$6

If you click on one of the ranges in the Consolidation Ranges List and then **Delete** you'll remove the range from the list.

The final step is to go to the worksheet where you want to put the result and click on the first cell where you want the results to be copied to:

For example, go to Total in the Worksheet tab  and then make sure you are editing the Copy Cell results box.

Copy results to:

- undefined -   ⌄ | I

Then click on the cell you want the results to be copied to:

	A	B	C	D	E
27					
28		Product	Retail Price	Sales	Total
29		Product 1			
30		Product 2			
31		Product 3			
32		Product 4			
33					
34					

You'll see the cell added to the box that you're editing:

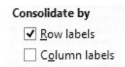

Click on ⊞ Options and make sure that you're consolidating based on rows and not columns in this case:

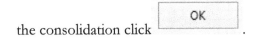

Obviously when you're consolidating a column you'll want to select the other option. When you're happy that you want to begin

the consolidation click   OK   .

So Long, and Thanks!

Writing this book has been great fun for me, and I hope that you've found it useful. As normal, I'd like to invite you to email me if you have any questions. My email address is thomasecclestone@yahoo.co.uk

LibreOffice Calc provides a fully functional spreadsheet without the cost of some of the alternatives. As you become familiar with it you'll probably find that it's a hugely powerful piece of software that will repay all the effort you've spent learning how to use it.

Finally, I'd like to thank you and wish you good luck!

ABOUT THE AUTHOR

Thomas Ecclestone is a software engineer and technical writer who lives in Kent, England. After getting his 1st class honours in software engineering he worked at the National Computing Centre in Manchester, the Manchester Metropolitan University, and for BEC systems Integration before starting his own business in software development. He is a writer who lives on a smallholding in Kent where he looks after a small flock of Hebridean sheep.

www.ingramcontent.com/pod-product-compliance
Lightning Source LLC
Chambersburg PA
CBHW071001050326
40689CB00014B/3449